The Faith Factor

Living Out What We Believe

Ed Miciano

WIPF & STOCK · Eugene, Oregon

Wipf and Stock Publishers
199 W 8th Ave, Suite 3
Eugene, OR 97401

The Faith Factor
Living Out What We Believe
By Miciano, Edoardo S.
Copyright©2010 by Miciano, Edoardo S.
ISBN 13: 978-1-5326-0952-7
Publication date 9/30/2016
Previously published by Bridgepoint Publishers, 2010

Unless otherwise indicated, all Scripture quotations are taken from
the *Holy Bible, New Living Translation*,
copyright © 1996. Used by permission
of Tyndale House Publishers, Inc.
Wheaton, Illinois 60189. All rights reserved

Scriptures marked "NIV" are taken from
the *Holy Bible, New International Version*,
copyright © 1973, 1978, 1984.
International Bible Society.
Used by permission of
Zondervan Bible Publishers.

Scriptures marked "TNIV" are taken from
the *Holy Bible, Today's New International Version*,
Copyright © 2001, 2005 by International Bible Society.

To my parents,

Tony and Cecille.

Thank you for raising me in a household of faith.

Acknowledgments

This book is the result of a sermon series that began the first Sunday of 2007 and ended five months later. I want to thank the awesome members of Bridgepoint Community Church for enduring through the series with me. You have made ministry work a joy and I am grateful for the opportunity to be your shepherd.

I also want to thank my dear friends, Jeff and Rhonda Angcanan, for assisting me in preparing the manuscript for publication. After all these years I can still count on you for help. I cherish our friendship and pray that in spite of our distance our paths might continue to cross often.

Finally, I am eternally grateful for my wife and kids. Thank you, Ana, for making our house a refuge that I enjoy coming home to. And to Jonathan, Rebekah, and Jacob, thanks for making fatherhood so much fun. I couldn't have asked for a greater set of descendants.

Contents

Prologue: What is Faith?	1
1. Abel: Honorable Faith	11
2. Enoch: Enduring Faith	21
3. Noah: Influential Faith	33
4. Abraham: Forward-Looking Faith	45
5. Abraham and Sarah: Persistent Faith	55
6. Abraham and Isaac: Tested Faith	65
7. Isaac, Jacob, and Joseph: Enduring Faith	75
8. Moses' Parents: Familial Faith	87
9. Moses: Independent Faith	97
10. The People of Israel (Part I): Courageous Faith	107
11. The People of Israel (Part II): Obedient Faith	117
12. Rahab: Gracious Faith	131
Epilogue: The Next Hero of Faith	139

prologue

What is Faith?

¹What is faith? It is the confident assurance that what we hope for is going to happen. It is the evidence of things we cannot yet see. ²God gave his approval to people in days of old because of their faith. ³By faith we understand that the entire universe was formed at God's command, that what we now see did not come from anything that can be seen.
(Hebrews 11:1-3)

Faith is a word that is used very commonly in modern culture. We talk about "keeping the faith" when enduring hard times. Politicians often take time to tell us about the role of their faith in office. Celebrities experiment with spiritual movements that help promote their choices as the next cool faith. Then, of course, there are the hundreds of world religions that deal with matters of faith.

So what is faith? I suppose there are a number of angles from which we could attempt to answer this question. Unfortunately, there isn't enough time and there aren't enough pages to cover such an exhaustive attempt. Let me then take one angle and modify the question this way: *What does the Bible say about faith?* And because even that is too broad a question, let us limit our discussion to a particular section of the Bible.

Hebrews 11, often described as Scripture's Hall of Fame of Faith, contains a wealth of information that provides us with a biblical worldview of faith. Here the author takes us through an historical journey unlike any other. By using narratives based on the lives of Old Testament characters, he allows to examine the issue of faith not merely as an intellectual proposition but as a matter of practical concern. Each character was a real, often simple, human being through whom God did great things primarily because they chose to put faith in Him. Although we may never converse with a burning bush, or slaughter a lion with a donkey jawbone, or even part the Red Sea, we can certainly relate to experiences such as crisis, frustration, persecution, familial discord, temptation, anger, loss, and pain. Herein lies the power of this great biblical chapter. Every faith experience described here finds a curious parallel with our own spiritual journey. As such, we read them with great interest and with a hope that as these ancient men and women were blessed to see the fruit of their faith, we too long to envision the fruit of ours.

Allow me then to unpack this great literary piece of luggage called Hebrews 11 by exploring its opening lines. Two questions will guide us in our effort to discover the riches of these words: 1) What is faith? and 2) How does faith work?

Let us begin by clarifying what faith is not. First of all, faith is not mere intellectual ascent. Knowing more about something does not necessarily translate into living out its implications. For instance, most people know that in order to live a healthy life, one must eat a sensible diet and exercise regularly. It would not be an exaggeration to assume that most adults in America are aware of this fact. Are we then a healthier country because of this knowledge? Not necessarily. On the contrary health and medical experts grieve over the fact that in spite of such knowledge, Americans today are not healthier than those a generation ago. In fact, we are far less healthy based on certain standards.

Secondly, faith is not superstitious anticipation. It is not wishing for something so badly and expecting it to come true purely on the basis of the intensity of that wish. While many believers cringe at the notion of being superstitious and even condemn any number of superstitious practices, I can't help but think that to some degree, all humans are superstitious. How many times have you found yourself in a Chinese restaurant opening a fortune cookie and wishing in your heart that it will spell out a favorable destiny for your life? We read something like, "You will amass a great amount of wealth in the near future" and deep inside we whisper, "Thank you, Jesus!" Irrational? Absolutely! Yet many of us do it. This, however, is not what the Bible calls faith.

Thirdly, faith is not self-confident assurance. Bible faith is not a matter of convincing yourself to believe something so strongly and expect it to come to fruition because of the strength of your confidence. Because faith is only as good as its object, the object of your faith must be one that is powerful enough to sustain your belief. And there is no greater object of faith than the Word of God.

The author of Hebrews offers a simple, yet profound definition of faith. He says, *Now faith is being sure of what we hope for and certain of what we do not see.*[1] In the New Living Translation, this same line reads, *It* (faith) *is the confident assurance that what we hope for is going to happen; It is the evidence of things we cannot yet see.* From this verse, we can draw two observations. One is that faith involves hope. Unfortunately, the English word for "hope" is far weaker than the original language connotes. In English, the word "hope" is more akin to "wish." However, the Bible word for hope, *elpis*, suggests more than just wishful thinking. Rather, it is characterized by a deep sense of confidence that what you expect

---

[1] Hebrews 11:1

to happen will transpire because God is more than capable of making it happen.

The second observation is that faith involves believing something even if we do not have immediate, tangible evidence available. It is almost analogous of going to work every day believing that at the end of the month, you will receive a paycheck. The check is not dangled before your eyes each working day. You simply trust that your employer is reliable enough to provide this compensation as agreed upon in your contract. Likewise, we believe in the promises of God even if it takes a while for that promise to be fulfilled. We hold on in faith because God's integrity is such that we can take Him at His Word. These two elements, hope in God and trust in God, constitute the biblical concept of faith.

So how does this kind of faith actually work? Four factors must be in place for Bible faith to function.

I. Revelation: Hearing the Word of God

The word *revelation* comes from a New Testament word from which we get the English word *apocalypse*. It literally means "to unveil something previously hidden." It conjures up the image of something valuable locked up on a chest, hidden from all to see. Then one day, someone with a key opens the chest and "reveals" the hidden treasure. This act of revealing is the work of God. While we often talk about discovering God's truths, the reality is that we can never discover what God has not first uncovered.

When my children were much younger, they would ask me to play hide-and-seek. They were so terrible at hiding. They chose all the wrong rooms and even when they found something to hide behind, they would always have an arm or limb extended far enough for me to see them. I, on the other hand, am a master hider. Being the genius that I am, I always managed to figure out where their childish curiosities would never think of looking. One particularly good hiding place was our coat closet. It was located at an obscure part of the house and my kids' feeble hands were not strong enough to open the closet door. Consequently, they never found me when it was my turn to hide. To alleviate their frustration, I would eventually leave the closet door ajar and stick out my arm for them to see. In no time at all, one of them would see my hand and shout, "Hey guys, come over here; I found dad!" But did they really find me? The fact is I allowed myself to be found by revealing a part of myself to them. In the same way, the only way to find God is for Him to show Himself to us. This is what we mean by revelation.

Faith begins when God reveals Himself to us through the Word. As the Apostle Paul put it, "Consequently, faith comes from hearing the message, and the message is heard through the word about Christ."[2] The Word is the object of our faith. The Bible reveals to us the person and nature of God and sets a foundation for us to put our hope and trust in Him. Evangelist D. L. Moody described it so well when he said, "I used to think I should close my Bible and pray for faith; but I came to see that it was in studying the Word that I was to get faith."

II.   Relationship: Walking with God

It is one thing to know about God, it is an entirely different thing to know God. I know about the current pope,

---

[2] Romans 10:17, TNIV

Pope Benedict XVI. I know a little bit about his career as a clergyman. I've browsed through some of his books. I've even seen him on television. But I don't know him. I simply do not have a relationship with him.

Do you know about God? Good. Do you have an opinion about him? Even better. That doesn't mean, however, that you have a relationship with Him. Knowing God is not a matter of reading a book or watching a documentary on the History Channel. Knowing God is about relating to Him at a very intimate level. The Bible uses the term "walking with God" to describe this kind of a relationship. Let me then ask a more important question: Are you walking with God?

Later in this book, you will learn about a man named Enoch. He walked so closely with God that the Bible says,

> After the birth of Methuselah, Enoch lived another 300 years in close fellowship with God, and he had others sons and daughters. Enoch lived 365 years in all. He enjoyed a close relationship with God throughout his life.[3]

Can you imagine being that close to God? We can only hope to be half the man of faith Enoch was.

You see, it is hard to trust someone you do not really know. Would you trust a stranger to watch your children? Or would you give an acquaintance power to manage your finances? Of course not! Then how can you entrust your very life and future to someone you don't even know?

How can we come to know God so well? As with any relationship, there is no substitute to spending a lot of time with

---

[3] Genesis 5:22-24

each other. In a marriage, for instance, couples soon discover that the concept of "quality time" can be a myth. Investing a hefty quantity of time is also necessary for the union to remain strong. And when we spend a good amount of time with someone, we begin to grow on each other, for better or for worse.

I recently read a story about Dr. Charles Weigle. He was in Pasadena once to attend a conference. During one break, he decided to visit the famous rose gardens of the city. Upon returning to the conference, one delegate remarked, "Ah, Dr. Weigle, you have just come from a visit to the rose garden!" "How did you know?", asked Weigle. The man replied, "Because I can smell the pleasing aroma of roses on your clothing." Does the "aroma" of God fill your life? Are you growing in your relationship with Him? Unless you are, you cannot fully function as a person of faith.

III. Response: Doing the Will of God

We do not always act on what we know to be true. Recently, a large athletic apparel company reported that ninety percent of people who buy running shoes don't actually run. For this large percentage of consumers, a running shoe is nothing more than a pricey fashion statement. Take the famous Nike Air Jordan for instance. At well over $100 a pair, you would think that wearing them would make you jump like Mike. In the mid 1980s, I put on one of the earlier Air Jordans. I could no more dunk a ball wearing them than I could barefoot. I soon discovered that if you want to play like Mike, you need to train like Mike. And train I never did. So much for that dream.

The Bible clearly says,

> Do not merely listen to the word, and so deceive yourselves. Do what it says. Those who listen to the word but do not do what it says are like people who look at their faces in a mirror and, after looking at themselves, go away and immediately forget what they look like. But those who look intently into the perfect law that gives freedom and continue in it—not forgetting what they have heard but doing it—they will be blessed in what they do.[4]

Bridging the divide between hearing the Word and doing the Word makes all the difference in the world when it comes to developing a faith that functions well.

In March, 1996, a 25 year old man named Roger Moore (not the actor) was given a ticket for not securing his toddler's car seat. He grumbled about the ticket while fastening his son into the appropriate restraint. Minutes later, his car was involved in an accident. His son, although bruised, was safe—but Roger died. He failed to put on his own seatbelt! Roger heard the "word" but didn't do anything about it for himself. Hearing the Word but not doing it can indeed have grave consequences.

IV. Reward: Enjoying the Blessings of God

A reward is a powerful motivator. A bodybuilder endures the pain of working out to reap the reward of a well-sculptured body. Students stay up late writing papers in order to march on stage and receive a diploma. Even a child will eat broccoli so that she might be treated to an ice cream sundae. So what does a person of faith get for exercising faith?

First of all, let me clarify that developing a close relationship with God is already a reward unto itself. Yet even

---

[4] James 1:22-25, TNIV.

God saw it in His heart to promise good things to those who remain strong in the faith. These promises are like signs posted intermittently along the freeway to remind us that our destination is getting closer as we travel. As tired as we might get, the words "next exit one mile" manages to bolster our energy and prod us to keep going until the journey is over.

Jesus gave us a glimpse of the journey's end. In one of the Gospels, Jesus spoke of how God will respond to a servant who was faithful until the very end: "His master replied, 'Well done, good and faithful servant! You have been faithful with a few things; I will put you in charge of many things. Come and share your master's happiness!'"[5] Every believer ought to live such faithful lives as to warrant receiving these same words from our Master. Richard Baxter, lamenting humanity's lack of passion for heavenly rewards, wrote:

> It is a most lamentable thing to see how most people spend their time and energy for trifles, while God is cast aside. He who is all seems to them as nothing, and that which is nothing seems to them as good as all. It is lamentable indeed, knowing that God has set mankind in such a race where heaven or hell is their certain end, that they should sit down and loiter, or run after the childish toys of the world, forgetting the prize they should run for. Were it but possible for one of us to see this business as the all-seeing God does, and see what most men and women in the world are interested in and what they are doing every day, it would be the saddest sight imaginable. Oh, how we should marvel at their madness and lament their self-delusion! If God had never told them what they were sent into the world to do, or what was before them in another world, then there would have been some excuse. But it is His sealed word, and they profess to believe it.

---

[5] Matthew 25:21, TNIV

I wish that we might be set free from lusting after the things that don't ultimately matter and instead, seek to live out our faith with our eyes fixed upon the eternal and heavenly gifts of God.

Everyone has a measure of faith. We all believe in something for some reason. The difference lies on the level upon which you exercise your faith. The Bible indicates that there are at least four levels of faith:
- No faith
- Little faith
- Faith
- Great Faith

As we journey together in the discovery of faith, may you find yourself moving up each level, one notch at a time.

chapter

1

ABEL: Honorable Faith

It was by faith that Abel brought a more acceptable offering to God than Cain did. God accepted Abel's offering to show that he was a righteous man. And although Abel is long dead, he still speaks to us because of his faith.
(Hebrews 11:4)

A few years ago, I received a call from my mother. "Your uncle just passed away," she said. I asked her what had happened and she explained that my uncle was shot by his own brother all because of a dispute regarding their family business. I was literally in shock because I could not comprehend how a man could pull a trigger at his own brother.

Don't get me wrong. I fully understand that in almost every family, siblings go through phases where they don't get along. I grew up with two brothers and we didn't always see things eye-to-eye. Speaking of eye, I remember when I was about four years old and my older brother was pestering me while I was eating. So I did the logical thing. I took the fork that was in my hand and threw it at him. The fork hit him just a hairline away from his eye. I can't even begin to describe how angry my mother was and I paid a price for it. But you don't know my brother. He deserved it as far as I was concerned.

Sibling rivalry is nothing new. It is as old as human history itself. The first brothers mentioned in the Bible, Cain and Abel, are a perfect example of this. You know how the story[1] goes. Abel outshines Cain, Cain is jealous of Abel, Cain kills Abel. But what about the story behind the story? A closer inspection of the Genesis narrative reveals that the sibling rivalry between Cain and Abel centered on the issue of faith, particularly as it related to their life of worship. Abel was a faithful man who worshiped God appropriately, whereas Cain was a faithless man who failed to honor God with his offerings.

Abel was somewhat of a pioneer. According to the biblical record, Abel was the first to be called a *man of faith*. He was the first to offer God an acceptable sacrifice in worship. He was the first to be called a *righteous man*. And he was the first to be killed because of his faith. He was quite a record-setter, wasn't he?

What is it exactly about Abel that makes him merit top billing in the Bible's Hall of Fame of Faith? An examination of Hebrews 11:4 reveals three fascinating facts about Abel's faith.

I. Abel's faith made him a better worshiper.

The Hebrew author notes that, "It was by faith that Abel brought a more acceptable offering to God than Cain did."[2] This assertion is based on the Genesis record that states:

---

[1] See Genesis 4:1-16
[2] Hebrews 11:4a

The Faith Factor

> In the course of time Cain brought some of the fruits of the soil as an offering to the Lord. But Abel brought fat portions from some of the firstborn of his flock. The Lord looked with favor on Abel and his offering, but on Cain and his offering he did not look with favor. So Cain was very angry, and his face was downcast.[3]

Abel teaches us that having faith enables us to live out our God-ordained purpose—to worship God sacrificially. He offered a worship sacrifice that was acceptable to God. But didn't Cain bring an offering to God as well? Why did he not receive the same response from the Lord? Scholars have suggested a number of possible reasons. Let me put forth the more plausible ones.

First of all, Abel's offering was the fruit of his labor. This was not a cheap gift. Abel was a shepherd by profession and he worked hard, day and night, to take care of his flock. He gave God an offering that represented the work of his hands. Abel teaches us that true worship involves sacrifice. We are not to simply offer God whatever happens to be around. Or worse, give to Him something we never worked for—a stolen offering, if you will.

In 1 Chronicles 21, King David was looking to purchase a piece of property where he could build an altar to the Lord. A man named Araunah offered his land for free but the King replied, "No, I insist on paying the full price. I will not take for the LORD what is yours, or sacrifice a burnt offering that costs me nothing."[4] Whether directly or indirectly, I believe that

---

[3] Genesis 4:3-5
[4] 1 Chronicles 21:24, NIV

Abel's life of worship had an influence on King David's attitude toward giving God a suitable offering.

Secondly, Abel offered the best of what he had. He didn't give God an ailing lamb or a sheep with a missing leg. The Bible says he brought "fat portions from some of the firstborn of his flock." Contrary to our modern aversion to fat, the ancients understood it to represent the best part of the animal. Furthermore, the giving of the firstborn was yet another indication that Abel did not withhold his best possible offering to God. Cain was a farmer and his offering to God came in the form of farm produce. Could it be that his offering did not represent the first fruits of his harvest? Could he have given the Lord rotten fruit, keeping the best ones for himself? The Bible doesn't say one way or another, but it certainly makes us curious.

When we give, we ought to give our best to God. A pastor from San Jose, California once told of a time when a member of his church drove up to the church driveway. On his truck's flatbed was a beat-up old couch which he wanted to donate to the church. He explained that he and his wife had bought a brand new couch, so they wanted to get rid of this old one by giving it as a charitable gift. The pastor responded, "Why don't you keep this old couch and give the new one to the Lord?" This story reminds me of the words of Mother Teresa who said, "If you give what you do not need, it isn't giving."

Thirdly, Abel's offering was acceptable because Abel himself was acceptable. Notice how the Bible says, "The Lord accepted Abel and his offering...."[5] So God accepted Abel first, and as long as Abel was acceptable, so was his offering. When you bring a gift to God, do you take time to first examine that

---

[5] Genesis 4:4b

your heart is right before Him? How many times have you offered worship to God only to realize that although there was nothing technically wrong with your gift, you yourself were not a fitting gift to the Lord? While God is certainly interested in the kind of offering you give, He is far more interested in the kind of person giving Him the gift. In his letter to the Romans, the Apostle Paul wrote, "I plead with you to give your bodies to God because of all he had done for you. Let them be a living and holy sacrifice—the kind he will find acceptable."[6]

II.   Abel's faith made him right before God.

The Hebrew writer goes on to say that, "God accepted Abel's offering to show that he was a righteous man".[7] Some have suggested that the reason Abel's gift was acceptable was because it involved the shedding of blood by an animal. Cain's offering, on the other hand, did not involve blood. Although I think there is some merit to this theory, the Bible does not clearly indicate that such was the case. It was as logical for a farmer to offer produce as it was for a shepherd to offer sheep. So that did not seem to be the problem.

Two passages give us a better clue as to why there was a discrepancy between God's responses to Cain and Abel. The first comes right out of the original account:

> Then the Lord said to Cain, "Why are you angry? Why is your face downcast? If you do what is right, will you not be accepted? But if you do not do what is right, sin is crouching at your door; it desires to have you, but you must master it.

---

[6] Romans 12:1
[7] Hebrews 11:4b

> Now Cain said to his brother Abel, "Let's go out to the field." And while they were in the field, Cain attacked his brother Abel and killed him."[8]

The second is written by the Apostle John:

> We must not be like Cain, who belonged to the evil one and killed his brother. And why did he kill him? Because Cain had been doing what was evil, and his brother had been doing what was right.[9]

According to these accounts, the crux of the issue was righteousness. Abel did what was right and good while Cain did what was wrong and evil. In the Bible, a righteous person is characterized by moral uprightness. It seems, therefore, that while many bring gifts to God in an attempt to become righteous, Abel gave an acceptable offering to God because he was already righteous.

The Bible teaches us that works of righteousness are not capable of helping us gain favor with God. All humans are sinners and are incapable of doing anything about this predicament. However, God, through the riches of His mercy and grace, saves us and makes us righteous through the death of Jesus Christ. Once we are saved, we perform works of righteousness, not in order to merit salvation, but as a testimony that we are truly saved.[10]

How did Abel become a righteous man? Theologically, he was not born righteous. The Apostle Paul reminds us that, "When Adam sinned, sin entered the entire human race. . . .

---

[8] Genesis 4:6-8
[9] 1 John 3:12
[10] See Ephesians 2:8-10

The Faith Factor

Adam's sin brought death, so death spread to everyone, for everyone sinned."[11] This teaching, known as the Doctrine of Original Sin, posits that all human beings are born as sinners because we all inherit the sinful nature of Adam. And guess who first inherited this nature? Cain and Abel, of course. So going back to the earlier question, how did Abel, a man sinful at birth, become a righteous man?

The Bible stipulates that it is the work of God to make us righteous. It does, however, remind us that we are to respond to this special work of grace. Abel gives us a clue as to how one ought to respond accordingly. First, he did what was right. He obeyed God's command to worship with clean hands and a pure heart. Second, he overcame his sinful inclinations. With the help of God, Abel did not allow his sinful nature to get the best of him. He did right and lived right in spite of the natural tendency to do wrong. And third, he lived by faith. It has been said that the step of faith must continue with the walk of faith. Abel showed us that it could be done.

Scripture reveals that righteousness is a result of the redemptive work of Jesus Christ at Calvary's cross. Jesus died in your place. Because He did, He is able to offer Himself as the perfect sacrifice to God in our behalf. If we accept His gift as our own, then we will share in the blessing of God's great salvation. Just as Abel put his faith in God, have you trusted Christ as your Savior and made a commitment to live by faith?

---

[11] Romans 5:12

THE FAITH FACTOR

III. Abel's faith made him speak beyond his grave.

The Hebrew author makes one more claim regarding Abel. He writes, "And although Abel is long dead, he still speaks to us because of his faith."[12] This is a reference to the statement made in Genesis:

> Then the Lord said to Cain, "Where is your brother Abel?" "I don't know," he replied. "Am I my brother's keeper?" The Lord said, "What have you done? Listen! Your brother's blood cries out to me from the ground."[13]

Thousands of years have passed since Abel died, yet he continues to speak to believers today. Interestingly, the Bible does not record a word spoken by Abel. Conversely, Cain's words are amply noted on the pages of Genesis. Yet it is the life message of Abel that continues to ring in the hearts of today's faithful.

How does Abel speak today? God said that his blood cries out from the ground. Blood represents life, and in a very real way, Abel's life teaches us how to live as a person of faith. Furthermore, Abel's life is what indicted his brother. He was not alive to testify against Cain's crime, but his blood was sufficient evidence that Cain was guilty. Finally, Abel's testimony continues to influence those of us who live in the present. I know many parents who name their children Abel, but I have yet to meet any who call their sons Cain.

A life lived out in faith becomes a legacy to others long after you have passed away. Think of how our lives today

---

[12] Hebrews 11:4c
[13] Genesis 4:9-10

continue to be touched by men and women who are no longer with us. We are indebted to Edison for the light bulb, to Ford for the automobile, to Bell for the telephone, to Guttenberg for printing, and to Abel for a great example of honorable faith.

I often wonder what kind of legacy I will leave my children. I can only hope that I live in such an honorable way that my blood will likewise be a witness to the grace and goodness of God. Only time will determine how you and I will be remembered. We can, however, make a wise decision today that will undoubtedly have an impact on the kind of heritage we bequeath to the generations that follow us.

What about you? What life message do people read in you? I pray that the life of Abel so inspires you to begin living a righteous life that brings glory to God your Creator. In that way, your faith will continue to influence others long after you are gone.

So what more can be said about these two famous brothers? In many ways, Cain and Abel were the same. They had the same parents, they grew up in the same environment, and they had similar religious practices. But in one critical way, they were different. Cain was a murderous sinner, while Abel was a righteous man. The legacy that each one leaves behind could not be any more different as well. I leave it up to you to decide in whose steps you will follow.

chapter

2

ENOCH: Enduring Faith

It was by faith that Enoch was taken up to heaven without dying—"he disappeared, because God took him." For before he was taken up, he was known as a person who pleased God. And it is impossible to please God without faith. Anyone who wants to come to him must believe that God exists and that he rewards those who sincerely seek him.
(Hebrews 11:5-6)

In my work as a pastor, I have officiated more funeral services than I care to remember. One of the most meaningful parts of a memorial service is the eulogy. This is a time when family and friends share their thoughts and feelings about the individual who has passed away. Each time I listen to a eulogy, I cannot help but think, "I wonder if the deceased knew what this person felt." Do you ever wonder what people will say about you when you die? I came across a story of one man who got a chance that few of us will ever have.

One morning in 1888, Alfred Nobel, inventor of dynamite, awoke to read his own obituary. The obituary was printed as a result of a simple journalistic error. You see, it was Alfred's brother who had died and the reporter carelessly reported the death of the wrong brother. Any man would be disturbed under the circumstances, but to Alfred, the shock was overwhelming because he saw himself as the world saw him. The "Dynamite King," the great industrialist who had made an immense fortune from explosives. This, as far as the general public was concerned, was the entire purpose of Alfred's life. None of his true intentions to break down the barriers that separated men and ideas for peace were recognized or given serious consideration. He was simply a merchant of death. And for that alone he would be remembered. As he read the obituary with horror, he resolved to make clear to the world the true meaning and purpose of his life. This could be done through the final disposition of his fortune. His last will and testament—an endowment of five annual prizes for outstanding contributions in physics, chemistry, physiology or medicine, literature, and peace (the sixth category of economics was added later)—would be the expression of his life's ideals and ultimately would be why we would remember him. The result was the most valuable of prizes given to those who had done the most for the cause of world peace. It is called today, the "Nobel Peace Prize."

Alfred Nobel got a second chance to ensure that his legacy would be positive and with long-lasting effects. Similarly, thousands of years ago, there was also a man who left us with an enduring legacy. We know him as Enoch. His is a fascinating story of how one can maintain a life of faithfulness even in the midst of difficult and trying times. The Book of Genesis provides us with a brief but poignant account of Enoch's life:

> When Enoch was 65 years old, his son Methuselah was born. After the birth of Methuselah, Enoch lived another 300 years in close fellowship with God, and he had other sons and daughters. Enoch lived 365 years in all. He enjoyed a close

relationship with God throughout his life. Then suddenly, he disappeared because God took him.[1]

Enoch lived in the years leading to the Noahic Flood. Those days were marked by rebellion, indecency, and wanton disregard for the commands of God. Even Jesus described those days as a time when "the people were enjoying banquets and parties and weddings right up to the time Noah entered his boat. . . . People didn't realize what was going to happen until the Flood came and swept them all away."[2] Normally, there would be nothing wrong with attending parties and wedding celebrations. But the people were doing so at a time when God had given a clear warning through Noah that a great act of judgment was to fall upon them. Their blatant disregard of such warnings was indicative of the callousness of their hearts. How difficult it must have been for Enoch to live as a man of faith during such a time.

How did Enoch do it? How did his faith endure such trying times? According to the accounts of his life in Genesis and Hebrews, Enoch lived through a faith experience that could be broken down into four identifiable phases.

I.   Enoch put his faith in God.

It is clear from both Genesis 5 and Hebrews 11 that Enoch was a man who had faith in God. He walked faithfully with God and eventually went to be with God by faith—or because of his faith. Enoch exemplified our earlier premise that the step of faith must continue with the walk of faith.

---

[1] Genesis 5:21-24
[2] Matthew 24:38-39

When did Enoch begin to live by faith? We get a clue from the words of the Genesis account. The writer noted that, "After he became the father of Methuselah, Enoch walked faithfully with God 300 years . . ."[3] Without trying to read too much into the text, it seems to me that Enoch began walking with God at the age of sixty-five. And the specific event tied to this momentous transformation was the birth of his son, Methuselah.

We are not told what exactly happened upon Methuselah's birth that would cause Enoch to begin living by faith. I can only venture to guess. I know for a fact that the birth of my firstborn, Jonathan, was a life-changing event for me. When I first held Jonathan in my hands, there was a definite shift in my thinking, my life commitment, and my sense of responsibility. In fact, someone shocked me that day when he said to me, "How does it feel holding the father of your grandchildren?" I had never thought of it that way before. I was completely overwhelmed, to say the least.

Perhaps Enoch felt the same way. The birth of his son may have reminded him of how life begins only to someday end. He might have thought of his own end. Was he indeed prepared to meet his Maker when that day came? What we do know is that from that time on, Enoch continued to walk in faith for the remainder of his earthly life.

You and I are not born believers. The Bible reminds us that, because of the fall of Adam, we are conceived in sin and therefore born as sinners.[4] Many people today may not believe that, but we will save that discussion for another time. Suffice it to say that as sinners, we eventually become believers at some

---

[3] Genesis 5:22, TNIV

[4] *For I was born a sinner—yes, from the moment my mother conceived me* (Psalm 51:5).

point after birth. The act or process of becoming a person of faith is often referred to as *conversion*. We convert (i.e., change) from becoming a sinner alienated from God, into a believer who walks with God. I refer to it as an act or process because, while there are those who can point to the specific moment when they began putting their faith in God, others experience a sequence of events leading to the conversion unto faith without being able to identify the precise moment when it occurred. In either case, the Bible acknowledges that both are equally valid conversions. What is important in both cases is that we act upon the Word of God and respond to Him by faith, as Jonathan Edwards explained:

> 'Tis not God's design that men should obtain assurance in any other way, than by mortifying corruption, and increasing in grace, and obtaining the lively exercises of it. And although self-examination be a duty of great use and importance, and by no means to be neglected; yet it is not the principal means, by which the saints do get satisfaction of their good estate. Assurance is not to be obtained so much by self-examination, as by action.[5]

Edwards asserts that gaining favor with God is not simply a matter of reflecting on one's spiritual condition. Many people lament their wicked ways, yet do nothing about it. Transformation takes place as we act on God's call to follow Him. We do this by putting faith in God.

---

[5] Jonathan Edwards, *The Religious Affections* (Yale University Press, 1950), p. 195.

II. Enoch lived in close fellowship with God.

The remaining 300 years of Enoch's life is described as a time of walking "in close fellowship with God."[6] In various parts of Scripture, *walking* is used as a euphemism for living and behaving. This means that Enoch not only proclaimed that he had faith in God. Rather, he behaved in such a way as to demonstrate that he was someone who was committed to living in close fellowship with God. This man was no hypocrite.

A hypocrite is a two-faced person. This imagery is derived from the literal origin of the word. In the Greek language a *hypocrite*[7] referred to an actor who was assuming the identity of a character other than himself. This was often done by wearing a theatric mask. That actor, therefore, had two "faces"—his actual face and the one on the mask. It was possible to look like a kind person, while in reality, be a ruthless individual. Religious people are often criticized, and rightly so, when they show off an aura of spirituality while living a life that is the very opposite.

The life of faith is not for the insincere. Living by faith means walking with God, and you cannot honestly walk with God without having an authentic relationship with him. Walking with God involves maintaining a life of prayer, regular Bible reading, fellowship with other believers, and communicating the love of God to others. It is a life of pure devotion. The great missionary, Adoniram Judson, asserted that, "The motto of every

---

[6] Genesis 5:22
[7] *Hupokrites*.

missionary, whether preacher, printer, or schoolmaster, ought to be 'Devoted for life.'"[8]

Is there any evidence in your daily life that you are walking close to God?

III.   Enoch learned how to bring pleasure to God.

Enoch not only walked with God, he pleased God. In Hebrews we read, "For before he was taken up, he was known as a person who pleased God."[9]   In contrast to the wickedness around him, Enoch's reputation as a God-pleaser set him apart from all the rest. There will be times when you are alone in your desire to please God. It is very tempting to take a step back and do what everyone else does in order to fit in. Don't give in to that temptation. Live for God and please Him alone. A dear pastor used to say to me, "When you please God, it doesn't matter who you displease; but if you displease God, it doesn't matter who you please."

As a post-graduate student, I was quite overwhelmed with all the writing requirements for the program. My first class was especially intimidating. When the term was over, we were given six months to complete a project paper. Six months went by and I wrote nothing!   I felt paralyzed.   I would sit behind the computer and nothing would come to my mind. An extension fee of $100 bought me another six months, and this time, I knew I had to get the work done. I expressed my difficulty to my professor and he asked me what the problem was. "I just don't think I can write a good enough paper," I replied. "Good enough

---

[8] Courtney Anderson, *To the Golden Shore: The Life of Adoniram Judson* (Judson Press, 1987).
[9] Hebrews 11:5

for whom?," he asked. "For others, I suppose," was my sheepish response. The good professor went on to remind me, "Ed, you are writing this paper for one person, and one person alone—me! Stop worrying about what other people will think and start concentrating on what I will think." Then, sticking out his index finger he said, "Miciano, write to an audience of one." That changed everything. Within two months, I completed my paper and submitted it well within the next deadline. Humility prevents me from telling you what grade I got. Let's just say it was a vowel grade, if you know what I mean.

Enoch did well because he lived only to please God. And how did he please God? By faith, of course. The author of Hebrews declares that, "without faith it is impossible to please God, because anyone who comes to him must believe that he exists and that he rewards those who earnestly seek him."[10] Faith brings pleasure to God. Better yet, faith is arguably the only thing that impresses God.

Have you thought about what makes God say *wow*? Think about it, what can we do to impress the Almighty Creator of the universe? God is not impressed by our rhetoric, or by our appearance, or even by our religiosity. But God is surely impressed by the gutsy exercise of faith. In the Gospel of Matthew, we read about a centurion who asked Jesus to heal his ailing servant. When Jesus offered to go to his home, the centurion responded, "Lord, I am not worthy to have you come into my home...Just say the word from where you are, and my servant will be healed!"[11] Matthew said that Jesus was *amazed*. It was as if Jesus' jaw dropped as He exclaimed, "I tell you the

---

[10] Hebrews 11:6
[11] Matthew 8:8

truth, I haven't seen faith like this in all the land of Israel!"[12] He essentially said, *Wow!*

We all live to please someone. We either live to please God, others, or ourselves. The problem with pleasing others is that you cannot please everyone all the time. The problem with pleasing only ourselves is that we become egocentric maniacs. Pleasing God, on the other hand, glorifies Him and brings about unspeakable blessings to us, and quite often, those around us as well.

IV. Enoch entered into the presence of God.

Because he believed in God, walked with God, and brought pleasure to God, Enoch was rewarded with the gift of eternal rest with God. His life story, however, ends in a very unusual way. In Genesis we read, "Then suddenly, he disappeared because God took him."[13] Likewise, in Hebrews, we are told that he was "taken up to heaven without dying."[14] Taken up without dying—how strange, and yet how wonderful! Can you imagine living in this world, then suddenly living with God in heaven in what must have appeared to be a seamless transition? I can't fully explain how something like that works, but I rather like the way one little girl explained it:

> A six-year-old girl came home from church and greeted her mother who was too ill to attend services that day. "How was Sunday School," the mother asked. "Wonderful, mom," she replied, "we learned about a man named Enoch." "Tell me about

---

[12] Matthew 8:10
[13] Genesis 24
[14] Hebrews 11:5

Enoch," said the mom. The girl explained, "One day, Enoch walked with God...and they walked, and they walked, and they walked. They walked all day, in fact. At the end of the day, it was dark and God said, 'Enoch, we are now too far for Me to send you to your house; why don't you just come home to Me?' And that's how Enoch went to live with God."

I'm not sure that that's how it happened, but it's as good an explanation as I've ever heard.

I assume that, with only a few exceptions, all people desire to go to heaven when they die. But wanting it badly enough is no guarantee that you will get what you want. Spending eternity with God is the result of walking with God upon receiving His gift of eternal life.[15] Ultimately, death has no power over a true believer—it is simply a door to an eternal existence with the God we love.

What will heaven be like? I don't know exactly. Other than what the Bible says, we know very little about it. One theologian, however, described it as an "unknown region with well-known inhabitants." We know at least one such inhabitant—Enoch. And if he represents the kind of people who will be there, then I certainly want to be there too.

Enoch was a man who pleased God because he lived by faith, he walked by faith, and he departed in faith. Are you trying to exercise enduring faith in the midst of difficult times? Let me leave you with the words of J. I. Packer who wrote, "To those who have learned to love and trust Jesus, the prospect of

---

[15] *But to all who believed him and accepted him, he gave the right to become children of God* (John 1:12).

meeting Him face to face and being with Him forever is the hope that keeps us going, no matter what life may throw at us."[16]

---

[16] James Packer, *Your Father Loves You* (Harold Shaw Publishers, 1986).

chapter

3

NOAH: Influential Faith

*By faith Noah, being warned by God about things not yet seen,
in reverence prepared an ark for the salvation of his household,
by which he condemned the world, and became an heir
of the righteousness which is according to faith.*
(Hebrews 11:7)

    The young boy just couldn't understand it. Why was his father asking the family to abandon their Jewish faith and start participating in the religious life of the Lutheran churches of Germany? When he asked this of his father, the old man simply replied, "This is what we must do in order for our business to survive in this country." This explanation never satisfied the lad. He would forever be bitter over his father's decision to change religions for purely commercial reasons.

    In time, he left Germany and moved to England where he studied at the British Museum. It was here that he espoused basic life principles that would serve as the foundation of his philosophy. He eventually wrote a book that embodied the spirit of his newfound worldview. We know this book as *The*

Communist Manifesto. And soon enough, Karl Marx would influence up to a third of the world with his political ideology—an ideology that led to unthinkable tragedies for 20th century Europe. All because of a father's failure to influence the faith of his son.

Faith is a personal matter, but it is not a private one. It is meant to be lived out in such a way that people are positively influenced by its precepts, and ultimately blessed by its outworking. Faith changes a person, and a person of faith changes the world. But before we succumb to delusions of grandeur, let us first consider how our faith changes the lives of those closest to us. Our faith ought to influence our family.

There was a man in Scripture who exemplified this principle. His name was Noah. We all know him as the great ark-builder. In fact, it is practically impossible to walk through the infant section of a department store without finding pillows, blankets, quilts, and other products depicting an old man in a boat surrounded by a zoo full of animals. He is known by both Biblicists and secularists. The story of Noah and the Flood supersedes Sunday School lectures and has infiltrated much of modern popular culture. Yet, there was more to boat-making than we give him credit for. Noah was primarily a man of faith.

The story of Noah is recorded in Genesis 6-9. Noah lived in a time of great wickedness. So wicked was the world that God determined to completely wipe out humanity from the face the earth. But the Lord could not annihilate the entire human race because there remained one faithful man. As an act of grace, God instructed Noah to build a large boat that would save them from a flood that would destroy all other living creatures. Because of Noah's faith, he was permitted to save others. In this case, his family, as well as a pair of every kind of animal. The rest, as we say, is history.

How did Noah develop such an influential faith? How could one man, living in such a wicked world, remain true to his faith and affect the lives of those dearest to him? A reading of Hebrews 11:7 gives us insight on the kind of faith Noah had.

I.   Noah's faith was an act of total surrender.

The first thing we are told about Noah is this: "By faith Noah, when warned about things not yet seen, in holy fear built an ark . . . ."[1] In Bible history, whenever God prepares to do something significant in the world, He begins with a person. In this case God began with Noah. The reason God chose him is because Noah "found favor with the Lord."[2] By this, we mean that the Lord looked upon him with special regard and thus, treated him with goodwill. We learn in Scripture that Noah gained this status in the eyes of the Lord because of his faith.

God communicated to Noah with words of warning and instruction. He was warned of the impending danger and then was instructed to build the ark as a means of living though the effects of the flood. Noah's response to God's word was to surrender totally to the Lord.

In one short phrase, the Hebrew author demonstrates how Noah involved his whole being in the act of surrender. First of all, Noah responded intellectually—he was *warned by God*. This means that as he reflected on God's warning, he aligned his thinking with the truth he heard.

---

[1] Hebrews 11:7a, NIV
[2] Genesis 6:8

Secondly, he responded emotionally—he acted in *holy fear*. Other versions of Scripture use the term *reverence*. To act with reverence means to be in awe of who God is and wholly submit to His requests. Such fear is not to be mistaken for terror. Rather, it has to do with quieting our thoughts and emotions and yielding them to God's will. This holy fear is born out of a sincere love for God.

Thirdly, Noah responded volitionally—he actually *built an ark*. The ultimate act of surrender was to pick up the hammer and begin building the ship that he was commanded to build. Often times we intellectually agree with God's precepts. We even respond emotionally to His presence. Yet in the end we never really do anything about it. This is not a true act of faith.

Think of the last sermon that impacted you. Were you convinced of its truth? Were you gripped by its passion? Did you actually put it to practice? Sadly, too many people forget this third all-important step. But not Noah. He heard it, he felt it, and he acted on it.

When we fully surrender to God, as Noah did, we do not have to fear what happens next because at that point, our lives are now in the hands of God. Andrew Murray once said, "God is ready to assume full responsibility for the life wholly yielded to Him." This is such a wonderful truth, and yet many of us still struggle with the issue of full surrender. In his book, *Believe and Belong*, Bruce Larson shares how he helps people deal with this inner conflict:

> For many years I worked in New York City and counseled at my office any number of people who were wrestling with this yes-or-no decision. Often I would suggest they walk with me from my office down to the RCA Building on Fifth Avenue. In the entrance of that building is a gigantic statue of Atlas, a

beautifully proportioned man who, with all his muscles straining, is holding the world upon his shoulders. There he is, the most powerfully built man in the world, and he can barely stand up under this burden. 'Now that's one way to live,' I would point out to my companion, 'trying to carry the world on your shoulders. But now come across the street with me.' "On the other side of Fifth Avenue is Saint Patrick's Cathedral, and there behind the high altar is a little shrine of the boy Jesus, perhaps eight or nine years old, and with no effort he is holding the world in one hand. My point was illustrated graphically. "We have a choice. We can carry the world on our shoulders, or we can say, 'I give up, Lord; here's my life. I give you my world, the whole world.'"[3]

With one act of total surrender, Noah shifted the weight of the world's wickedness from his shoulder to the hand of God.

II. Noah's faith had an impact on his family.

The Bible says that Noah built the ark *to save his family*. The Genesis account does not mention anything about the faith of Noah's wife, his sons, and his daughters-in-law. All we know is that Noah himself was a man of faith. The text asserts that, "Noah was a righteous man, the only blameless man living on the earth at the time."[4] It was to him that the blessing of salvation from the flood was given as a gift of God. But as part of that blessing the Lord promised, "Everything on earth will die . . . .But I solemnly swear to keep you safe in the boat, with your wife and your sons and their wives."[5] Remarkably, Noah's

---

[3] Bruce Larson, *Believe and Belong* (Power Publications, 1982).
[4] Genesis 6:9
[5] Genesis 6:17-18

family was saved even though he alone was identified as the person of faith.

Theologically, faith is not transferrable. Every human is individually responsible for having faith or the lack thereof. However, faith can and must be contagious. Earlier, we asserted that although faith is personal, it is not private. The effects of our faith flow out of our being and touch the lives of those around us. The effects of Noah's faith clearly spilled over to his family, resulting in their own deliverance from the flood.

In the book of Acts, we read about a Philippian jailer who asks Paul how he might be saved. Paul replied, "Believe on the Lord Jesus and you will be saved, along with your entire household."[6] Let us be clear that Paul was not giving a magical formula on how to save everyone in your family. By believing on the Lord, the jailer would not automatically save his household. What it means is that once the man believes on Christ, it is assumed that he will begin living out his faith, through word and deed, in such a way that will influence members of his household to likewise put their faith in God. Faith, therefore, necessarily involves a missional element. We believe not only for our sake, but also for the sake of others.

My parents are an excellent example of this. In 1981, my mom and dad believed in the Lord and began their journey of faith. It was not long before they began telling my brother and me about what God did in their lives. They spoke God's Word incessantly and began to demonstrate meaningful changes in their behavior. They started taking us to a church where the Gospel message was preached clearly and unashamedly. Within a few weeks, my older brother and I also put our faith in Christ.

---

[6] Acts 16:31

A few years later, my younger brother who was just a toddler then, eventually came to Christ as well. My parents reaped the promise that God would save their "household" because they dared to live out their faith each day.

Are you a person of faith? Is it contagious? What evidence is there that your faith is influencing the people around you? Noah believed the Lord and his family members were saved as a result.

III.   Noah's faith exposed human sinfulness.

Faith is a double-edged sword. It magnifies the righteousness of God in our lives, yet at the same time, it exposes the evil in others. The Bible says that, "By his (Noah's) faith he condemned the world."[7] Keep in mind that the people of the world were exceedingly wicked. That is why God was about to destroy it. But God couldn't just destroy people without giving them any warning. The warning came by way of Noah's life. There is no record of Noah ever saying, "I condemn you," to the people in his generation. But we do know that, "Noah warned the world of God's righteous judgment."[8] We don't know if he did this through words, but he certainly did it through deeds.

Here in Northern California, winter brings extended periods of rain. During this time, it really doesn't make sense to wash your car until the season is over. Eventually, all cars become muddy and dirty. Then one day, someone will be the first to get a car wash. This lone clean car roams the freeway amidst thousands of filthy cars. Without saying a word, this car

---

[7] Hebrews 11:7
[8] 2 Peter 2:5

condemns the dirty condition of all the others. Its shiny body and clear windshield exposes how filthy all other cars are. And all it has to do is be the clean car that it now is. Likewise, Noah condemned the world by staying clean (i.e. holy) in a wicked environment.

One day, St. Francis invited young monks to town in order to preach the Gospel. A young novice monk was excited to be singled out as Francis' companion. As they entered the town, they walked through the market, down the town square, and along the neighborhood streets. They then returned back to the monastery. The young monk was puzzled. He was certain they went to town in order to preach the Gospel, yet neither he nor Francis ever said a word. He mustered enough courage to ask the senior monk, "Have you forgotten that we were supposed to preach?" Francis then offered this famous reply:

> My son, we have preached. We were preaching while we were walking. We have been seen by many; our behavior has been closely watched; it was thus that we have preached our morning sermon. It is of no use to walk anywhere to preach unless we preach everywhere as we walk. Preach the Gospel always, and if necessary, use words.

We can only imagine the ridicule Noah suffered from wicked people as he faithfully built the ark. After all, how foolish it would have seemed to watch a 500-year-old man building a large boat in the middle of dry ground. But Noah pressed on for one hundred years until the day of the flood. He preached through his life of obedience to God. And when the destruction came for the world, no one could say that they did not have ample warning.

IV. Noah's faith earned eternal rewards.

The immediate result of Noah's faithfulness is that he and his family were spared from the flood-caused destruction of the world. There was, however, a more lasting result. The Bible says that Noah "became heir of the righteousness that comes by faith."[9] All in all, Noah reaped a threefold reward. First, he was spared from the flood. Second, he was commissioned to replenish the human population. And third, he went on to live eternally in God's presence reaching the inheritance of righteousness.

Bible faith is not one-dimensional in its results. Even though we exercise faith in one particular area of life, it often manifests itself in every other aspect of our existence, including our eternal existence. A perfect example of this is the phenomenon known as *redemption and lift*. This theory, made popular by Donald McGavran and C. Peter Wagner,[10] suggests that when an individual receives Christ as Lord and Savior, his or her blessing is not limited to eternal life in heaven. Rather, this redemption also causes a *lift*, so to speak, in other areas of life.

Take for instance a man who has so succumbed to a life of drunkenness that it causes him his family and his job. At an inner-city rescue mission, he gets a warm meal while listening to the Gospel message. So convicted is he that he surrenders his life to Christ. At that point, this man is redeemed, that is, his life is bought through the blood of Christ and is now rewarded with the gift of eternal life in heaven. But not only that. In the process of spiritual transformation, this man overcomes his

---

[9] Hebrews 11:7, NIV
[10] Donald Anderson McGavran and C. Peter Wagner, *Understanding Church Growth* (Wm. B. Eerdmans Publishing Company, 1990).

drinking addiction, sobers up, and cleans up. Soon he lands a stable job and reenters society as an upstanding citizen. Later, he even finds a Christian woman who shares her life with him through a committed marriage. This marriage is blessed with children who are raised in a godly environment. And on and on the blessings come. These blessings or *lifts* are the byproduct of the original faith encounter—believing on the Lord Jesus.

Sometimes, people of faith are accused of following God only for the rewards. C. S. Lewis responds to such accusations with this remark:

> We must not be troubled by unbelievers when they say that this promise of rewards makes the Christian's life a mercenary affair. There are different kinds of reward. There is the reward which has no natural connection with things you do to earn it, and is quite foreign to the desires that ought to accompany those things. Money is not the natural reward of love; that is why we call a man mercenary if he marries a woman for the sake of her money. But marriage is the proper reward for a real lover, and he is not mercenary for desiring it.[11]

Our relationship with God and its subsequent rewards are the result of a loving relationship with our Savior Jesus Christ.

The name "Noah" means "rest" and "quiet." What an ironic moniker for someone who lived through one of the most tumultuous period of human history. Yet Noah was indeed at rest—he rested on the promises of God and was thus spared from destruction.

God wants to give you rest. Not a momentary period of relaxation. Rather, a life of tranquility based on the assurance

---

[11] Quoted from Ken and Barbara Hughes, *Liberating Ministry from the Success Syndrome* (Crossway Books, 2008).

that, no matter what transpires in this life, we will always be safe with God for all eternity because of the sacrificial death of our Savior Jesus Christ.

chapter

4

ABRAHAM: Forward-looking Faith

By faith Abraham, when called to go to a place he would later receive as his inheritance, obeyed and went, even though he did not know where he was going. By faith he made his home in the promised land like a stranger in a foreign country; he lived in tents, as did Isaac and Jacob, who were heirs with him of the same promise. For he was looking forward to the city with foundations, whose architect and builder is God.
(Hebrews 11:8-10)

A small-town television news program reported on a local resident who was celebrating his 100th birthday. The reporter worked his way to the celebrant, stuck a microphone to his mouth and asked, "What is the secret to living long?" The old man simply replied, "Don't die."

How we wish it were that simple. There is obviously more to living long than simply not dying. However, the fact remains that as long as we don't die, we will continue to age. Unfortunately, in today's culture, many look down on growing old. Cosmetic counters are full of products that promise to defy age, health stores peddle supplements that are designed to slow down the effects of aging, and countless other industries exist to address the evils of growing old. Then, of course, there are all the jokes that have to do with, shall we say, maturing. Here are a few of my favorites:

You know you are getting old when:
- You are asleep but others worry that you are dead.
- You throw a wild birthday party in your home and the neighbors don't even notice.
- You feel pain in every part of your body—and the parts that don't hurt don't work.
- Your best friend is dating a lady half his age and it's not illegal.
- You bend to pick up something on the floor and while you're down there, you look for other things to pick up to save you the trip.
- You get a call at 7:00 p.m. and the person says, "Oh sorry, did I awake you?"
- You use the word "grass" to actually refer to the stuff on your lawn.

I could go on forever but I think you get my point. Getting old can be funny but it isn't always fun. The good news is, your age has little to do with whether or not God can still use you for His glory. Case in point? Father Abraham.

Abraham is arguably one of the most revered figures in all of human history. He holds a special place in the hearts of three great religious systems: Judaism, Islam, and Christianity. He is often referred to as Father Abraham because both Arabs and Jews are said to be his direct descendants. And although many Christians have neither a Jewish nor Arabic heritage, they still revere Abraham as their Father in the Faith.

THE FAITH FACTOR

Not much is known of Abraham's childhood and early life. In fact, the first time we meet him in the Bible, he is already about seventy-five years old—long past the retirement age by modern western standards. Yet at seventy-five, God was only about to begin his work through this man. In effect, Abraham teaches us that it is never too late to live a life of faith for the honor of God.

If I could use a term to describe Abraham's faith, I would say *forward-looking*. I find this to be notably unusual because most elderly people tend to be backward-looking. They are mostly focused on the past and constantly talking about the good-old days. But not Abraham. At seventy-five years of age, he began a forward-looking journey of faith that would last another one hundred years![1]

The author of Hebrews reveals three remarkable facts about Abraham's forward-looking faith.

I. Abraham obeyed God wholeheartedly.

We first meet Abraham in Genesis 12. His original name was Abram, meaning "high father." Abram was originally from an area called Ur of the Chaldeans, a city close to the banks of the Euphrates River in Mesopotamia, known today as modern-day Iraq.

The opening verses of chapter 12, as well as other Old Testament passages, reveal some very interesting facts about Abram[2] and his call. First of all, as noted earlier, he was seventy-five years old when God called him. We also discover

---

[1] Genesis 25:7
[2] Abram was Abraham's pre-covenant name.

that he was an idol-worshiper[3] at the time God spoke to him. Finally, he was a wealthy man who was fairly well-situated in his hometown. Think about it. God called a rich, old pagan to become the father of a new and great nation. Very unusual, to say the least.

Equally interesting are the conditions surrounding Abraham's call and response. The Hebrew author wrote, "It was by faith that Abraham obeyed when God called him to leave home and go to another land that God would give him as his inheritance. He went without knowing where he was going."[4] The Lord chose Abram to be the father of a new nation. This meant that he had to leave his homeland and relocate to a new land promised to him by God.[5] This new nation of people would be so great that they are likened to the stars in the sky. To mark this covenant promise, Abram's name would be changed to Abraham, meaning "father of a multitude."[6]

Amazingly, Abraham obeyed God even when he had many reasons to disobey. When God told him to leave his home he could have argued that he was too old and was already comfortable where he lived. When God asked him to go to another land that would be given as an inheritance, he could have reasoned that he did not need an inheritance because he was already rich. Even more, he could have resisted the idea of going somewhere without even knowing where that somewhere was.

I left my home at the age of twenty-one. After completing my college degree in Manila, I had the opportunity to come to America to go to graduate school. Although the U. S.

---

[3] Joshua 24:2
[4] Hebrews 11:8
[5] Hence the term, "Promised Land."
[6] Genesis 17:1-5

was a foreign land, I was not completely in the dark about where I was going. I knew what school I was attending, I had a plane ticket that would get me there, and I had friends who made arrangements to receive me when I arrived. It was not a very difficult trip at all.

Abraham had none of that. He did not know where he was going, he did not know how to get there, and he did not know how long the journey would take. All he knew is that God told him to go. His was not a cautious kind of obedience. Rather, it was remarkably swift. No arguments, no second-thoughts—just outright obedience.

In medicine, reflex action refers to an instantaneous movement in response to a stimulus. Doctors often test a patient's reflex action by striking a small hammer to the knee. Under normal circumstances, the lower leg will jerk almost as soon as the knee is struck. The absence of a reaction could indicate a potential medical problem. Spiritually speaking, God often tests our obedience reflex. The obedience reflex refers to the time it takes between hearing a command and responding to it. In Abraham's case, his obedience reflex was very quick. It is almost as if he snapped to attention immediately after God made his directive known.

Some of us, on the other hand, suffer from slow reflexes. It takes almost forever for us to obey a clear command from God. Or worse, we do not respond at all. We make too many excuses for not obeying immediately. It's not the right time, it's just too hard, it will cost too much, what will people think, and on and on our excuses pile up. A wise man once told me that delayed obedience is no obedience at all. We either obey God wholeheartedly or not. Abraham trusted in God with everything he owned and, as a result, he was blessed beyond anything he could ever imagine.

II.   Abraham lived on earth transiently.

After Abraham left Ur, he eventually arrived in the land of Canaan. In Hebrews we read, "And even when he reached the land God promised him, he lived there by faith—for he was like a foreigner; living in a tent. And so did Isaac and Jacob, to whom God gave the same promise."[7] This passage, along with Genesis 12:5-9, reveals that Abraham did two things that would characterize his journeys. First of all, wherever he went, Abraham pitched a tent. It is interesting how such a wealthy man never built a house, but instead, lived in tents for the remainder of his earthly life. Second, before he would break camp and travel to the next stop, he would build an altar. On this altar, he would offer a sacrificial gift to God as an act of worship and thanksgiving. Abraham was a spiritual sojourner. He lived in a tent, but he worshiped by an altar.

The tent was made of cloth and was portable, while the altars were made of stone and were permanent. The tent represented Abraham's status as a pilgrim while the altar represented his status as a worshiper. He did not build a house because this world was not his home. However, everywhere he went, he made sure to leave a memorial to God's greatness. As subsequent travelers would trek through the same land, there would be no evidence of where Abraham lived, but there would be multiple evidences of where he worshiped.

---

[7] Hebrews 11:9

The Faith Factor

I wonder if you and I are guilty of living in an opposite manner. Too often, our earthly residence is permanent while our worship life is transient. We are too preoccupied with amassing material goods with little attention to our spiritual growth and relationship with God. Many of us begin the journey with the right intentions, but soon we are so enamored by the things of the world that we simply lose sight of where it is we should be going. We collect things that have no eternal value. We invest in the temporal only to discover that our investments eventually perish with time. Imagine how different your life would be if you invested your time, abilities and resources to a cause that is eternal. What is keeping you from actually living this way?

A young adventurer decided to hitchhike across Europe one summer. Upon reaching the mountainous region in Germany, he happened upon a small monastery. Out of curiosity, he knocked on the massive wooden door and was welcomed by an elderly monk. The monk invited the traveler in to his residence in order to rest and enjoy a cup of tea. The young man could not help notice that all the monk had was an old bed, a study table and some books. "Where is the rest of your furniture?" he asked. The monk replied, "I don't have more furniture." The sage went on to ask, "And what about you, my son, where is *your* furniture?" The young man answered, "I don't need furniture because I don't live here; I am merely a traveler." To which the monk replied, "So am I, my son, so am I."

There is nothing necessarily wrong with owning things but there is something wrong with clinging to earthly goods as if we could not live without them. People of faith live transient lives. We do not hold tightly to material wealth because we know that all physical riches will not last forever. Traveling with too much baggage only makes the journey more difficult. This unnecessary weight slows down our attempt to reach our God-directed destination. If we are not careful, this weight might even cause us to lose our faith altogether.

III. Abraham looked to the future expectantly.

Abraham lived on earth as a foreigner because he had his eyes on a more glorious land. The Hebrew author wrote, "Abraham did this because he was confidently looking forward to a city with eternal foundations, a city designed and built by God."[8] He left so much in Ur—his family, his friends, his land, his memories. But Abraham did not look back. At no point did he decide to abort his journey and return to his old home. Even when he faced trials and difficulties, he refused to let his thoughts dwell on the "good old days." Years later, Abraham would seek a wife for his son, Isaac, from among the Chaldeans. Yet in doing so, he instructed his servant to return to Ur without taking Isaac back there.[9] Instead, the chosen wife would be brought to Isaac in Canaan. Abraham determined that he and his descendants would never go back.

The 15th century Spanish conquistador, Hernando Cortez, led the expedition that caused the fall of the Aztec Empire. Upon landing on the shores of Mexico, he ordered all their ships burned in order to eliminate the option of returning home to Spain without completing the mission. With the ships gone, Cortez and his men were left with no other option than to

---

[8] Hebrews 11:10
[9] Genesis 24:6

complete the work they set out to do. In the same way, Abraham *burned his ships* when he left Ur.

Instead of looking back, Abraham looked forward. Particularly, he was looking forward to a land far greater than the one he left. He journeyed to the Promised Land with an eye towards heaven, gazing at a city with "eternal foundations, a city designed and built by God."

I am fortunate to live by one of the most beautiful cities in the world. San Francisco is known for its beautiful landscapes, marvelous bridges, and all-year perfect climate. Every visitor I know cannot help but be enthralled by its magnificence. But even this City by the Bay is no match for what heaven must look like. I can't even begin to describe it to you, but I can only imagine how wonderful it would look like since God Himself is its architect and builder.

Heaven must be glorious in its beauty, for how can God create anything less? Best of all, God Himself is there. I suppose this is what Abraham really had his eye on. A dear friend of mine owns a beautiful home. Yet, whenever I visit him I am less interested in what his house looks like (which is impeccable) and am more interested in meeting him. Living where God dwells must be a mind-boggling experience. But more marvelous is the thought of being in the presence of my Creator and my Savior for all eternity. It is no wonder that Abraham had his eye on God's city even as he walked this earth with many blessings.

In 1895, the city of Leadville, Colorado witnessed the building of the largest ice palace in America. The palace was built to give the local economy a boost by attracting tourists. The massive structure which measured 450 by 320 feet was lined with towers that rose ninety feet in the air. The interior even had a 16,000 square foot skating rink. But alas, when winter was over the entire palace began to melt until nothing was left except a large puddle. Soon, all the shopping, the skating, the sightseeing and the excitement came to a screeching halt in the little town of Leadville. The world as we know it will likewise face this inevitable end. What a sad day it will be for those who lived as if this was all there was to live for. But for those who live by faith, the end of this life simply marks the beginning of an even greater one. Abraham lived a long and fruitful life, but his physical death was merely a transition into a more meaningful existence. An eternity with his Lord and Savior.

Are you a "forward-looking" person? Are you still expectant of Christ's glorious return? Does your attitude in life reflect this expectation? As you travel through life's journey, I encourage you to take your eyes off the things of this world and keep your eyes on Jesus.

chapter

5

Abraham and Sarah: Persistent Faith

> *[11] By faith Abraham, even though he was past age—and Sarah herself was barren—was enabled to become a father because he considered him faithful who had made the promise. [12] And so from this one man, and he as good as dead, came descendants as numerous as the stars in the sky and as countless as the sand on the seashore.*
> (Hebrews 11:11-12)

On December 30, 2006, ABC International reported this unbelievable story:

> A 67-year-old Spanish woman became the world's oldest mother after she gave birth to twins in the northern city of Barcelona on Saturday, a hospital official said. The woman, whose identity has not been revealed by Sant Pau hospital, gave birth by caesarian section on Saturday, having previously undergone in vitro fertilization in the United States, according to the national news agency EFE. Originally from the southern region of Andalucia, the new mother chose the Barcelona hospital because it specializes in high-risk births. The mother and twins are all doing well, though the babies are both in incubators, a hospital spokeswoman said. The hospital did not

reveal the gender of the twins. The previous holder of the oldest mother record was 66-year-old Romanian citizen Adriana Iliescu who gave birth to baby Eliza Maria in Jan. 2005.

Anyone who understands the intricacies involved in the birth of a human being appreciates how remarkable this story is. Amazingly, there is a story of another woman who became a mother at a much later age. Her name was Sarah, the wife of Abraham. In the record of faithful people, Sarah is listed along with her husband as a person who received God's blessing by faith.

In the previous chapter, we learned about how God called Abraham to be the father of a new nation at the age of seventy-five. Logically this meant that Sarah, who was about ten years younger than Abraham, would be the mother of this new nation. But in order for this to happen, they needed nothing less than a miracle.

Faith thrives in an environment of crisis. And Abraham and Sarah were certainly in a crisis. How could they be parents of a great nation when all the odds were stacked against them? How could God possibly make a way? Is there a point where even faith is no longer a logical option? Let us examine this couple's faith journey to see how God fulfilled his promise to them against all odds.

I.   Abraham and Sarah experienced the impossible.

The passage in Hebrews begins by saying, "By faith Abraham, even though he was past age—and Sarah herself was

THE FAITH FACTOR

barren—was enabled to become a father...."[1] I know exactly how my wife and I became parents (I will spare you the details). But Abraham and Sarah became parents primarily *by faith*. Why so? Because Sarah, the future mother of God's new people, had a problem. To be precise, she had two.

First of all, Sarah was old. At sixty-five, it made little sense that she would still be capable of bearing a child. In the ancient world, women tended to marry and have children much earlier than they do in modern times. It was not unusual then for girls to start raising a family in their teenage years. The concept of adolescence was virtually nonexistence in the ancient world. Males moved from boyhood to manhood at around twelve or thirteen. They would typically be married by the time they were sixteen or seventeen. Females, likewise, became women when they reached the age of thirteen or fourteen. Since women were not expected to go to school and prepare for a career, they were poised to get married and start having children at that young age. As a father of a pre-teen daughter, I'm glad times have changed! But can you imagine how old Sarah must have felt when faced with the notion that she would be a brand new mom at sixty-five? It was almost unthinkable.

Sarah had a second problem. She was barren. This was clearly the more difficult dilemma of the two. Barrenness refers to the general medical condition wherein a woman is not capable of conceiving a child. It is not at all an unusual condition as many women today continue to deal with infertility. In Biblical times, however, barrenness was not simply a medical condition. To many ancients, it was a curse. The closing of a woman's womb was interpreted to be an act of God. It was punishment for

---
[1] Hebrews 11:11a

sin. Socially, it was shameful to be known as a barren woman. People just naturally assumed that there was something morally wrong with you if you were unable to bear a child. No wonder many barren women in Scripture are described as woeful or remorseful.

It seemed like Sarah was willing to believe God in spite of her problems. But ten years later, she started to get impatient. She began to have doubts regarding God's promise. Here she was, now a seventy-five year old barren woman still expecting God to give her a child. Then she began to rationalize the situation. She may have argued that although God called her husband to be the father of a nation, He did not necessarily specify that she would be the mother. Could it be that God intended to use another woman to bear Abraham's child? According to Genesis 16, she proceeded with a new scheme.

Sarah went to Abraham and proposed that he sleep with her servant, Hagar, in order to expedite God's promise. She told her husband, "The LORD has kept me from having any children ... Go and sleep with my servant. ... Perhaps I can have children through her."[2] Abraham surprisingly obliged and soon Hagar was pregnant. Unfortunately, things didn't go as planned.

When Hagar knew that she was carrying Abraham's child, she started to taunt Sarah. We are not told exactly what she did or said, but we can only imagine how she used her pregnancy to make Sarah envious and drove her to anger and self-pity. Sarah was so upset that she even blamed Abraham for her troubles. She said,

---

[2] Genesis 16:2

THE FAITH FACTOR

> It's all your fault! . . . Now this servant of mine is pregnant, and she despises me, though I myself gave her the privilege of sleeping with you. . . . The Lord will make you pay for doing this to me![3]

Poor Abraham. He was just being an obedient husband. Now he was caught between two feuding women—the one who bore his child and the one he loved. Not wanting to dig a deeper hole, Abraham gave Sarah permission to treat Hagar as she wished. Sarah treated her harshly and soon Hagar ran away. Sarah's impatience with the promise of God came back to bite her in more ways than she expected.

Hagar eventually gave birth to a son, Ishmael. He was Abraham's firstborn, yet it became clear that it would not be through him that the promise would be fulfilled. This left Abraham and Sarah back to where they were, in need of a miracle. Only now, Sarah was even much older and her barrenness remained an issue.

Are you in need of a miracle? Consider yourself in good company. Do you believe a miracle is possible? You are in good company as well. A survey by the Princeton Religion Research Center revealed that 82% of adults believed that "even today, miracles are performed by the power of God."[4] It is always too early to give up on your faith. Abraham and Sarah will soon learn how true that is.

---

[3] Genesis 16:5
[4] PRRC Emerging Trends.

II.   Abraham and Sarah experienced God's faithfulness.

The Bible says that Abraham and Sarah were primed for a miracle because he considered Him faithful who made the promise.[5] You see, the power of God's promise is not so much grounded on your ability to believe in it as much as on the faithfulness of God to fulfill it. It will happen because God said it will happen. His track record is impeccable.

If you think it was hard for Sarah to believe that God could make her a mother at seventy-five, then brace yourself. God would actually make her wait another fourteen years before finally fulfilling the promise.

Genesis 18 records the events surrounding Sarah's pregnancy. One unassuming day, Abraham was going about his business when three men came to visit him. Abraham invited them to rest and be refreshed from their travels as he asked Sarah to prepare them a meal. In the course of their conversation, one of the men said to Abraham, "About this time next year I will return, and your wife Sarah will have a son."[6] Abraham must have been excited. After almost twenty-five years of waiting upon the Lord, this was the most specific prophecy given regarding the time he and Sarah would become parents. Sarah, on the other hand, had a slightly different reaction. The Bible said that she heard the man's words and then laughed silently to herself. She reasoned, "How could a worn-out woman like me have a baby?. . . And when my master—my husband—is also so

---

[5] Hebrews 11:11b
[6] Genesis 18:10

old?"[7] The visitor heard her faint laughter and then offered a gentle rebuke:

> Why did Sarah laugh? Why did she say, "Can an old woman like me have a baby?" Is anything too hard for the LORD? About a year from now, just as I told you, I will return, and Sarah will have a son.[8]

Sure enough, the Lord fulfilled his promise and less than a year later, Isaac was born. Upon giving birth, Sarah cried out, "God has brought me laughter! All who hear about this will laugh with me. For who would have dreamed that I would ever have a baby? Yet I have given Abraham a son in his old age!"[9] Sarah laughed, but this time, it had a noticeably different tone. Hers was no longer a laughter of curiosity but one of great joy. There is little that can match the feeling of holding your first child in your hands. That feeling must definitely be heightened when you are a ninety-year-old woman looking at your firstborn son.

Just picture your grandmother or great-grandmother and imagine her holding a newborn child. Ridiculous, isn't it? Only a miracle would make that possible. And a miracle is exactly what Abraham and Sarah got. They were rewarded with such a wonderful gift because they had faith.

Too often, we minimize our expectation of God's faithfulness when we maximize the appearance of our crisis. It could very well be that Christ is already at work in your situation but you are so focused on the problem that you fail to see what

---

[7] Genesis 18:12
[8] Genesis 18:13-14
[9] Genesis 21:6-7

he is doing. How many times have we missed out on a mighty move of God simply because our gaze was fixed elsewhere? Don't fall for that mistake again. Stay focused on God's Word and his promises because they are forever sure.

Faith was the operating principle in Abe and Sarah's miracle. They were blessed by God because they believed God. Are you continuing to believe God even when things are not going your way? Keep in mind that your crisis will not last forever but the Lord is an everlasting God. You will never experience his faithfulness until you hang around long enough to see his works unfold. It might happen when you least expect it, and when it does, just consider it one of God's pleasant surprises.

III. Abraham and Sarah experienced the power of resurrection.

From the standpoint of medical reproduction, Abraham and Sarah were "dead." Couples their age are normally no longer expected to have children, much less their first child together. Yet the Hebrew author reminds us, "And so from this one man, and he as good as dead, came descendants as numerous as the stars in the sky and as countless as the sand on the seashore."[10] Even the writer was so amazed with Abraham's age that he described him as "good as dead." The miracle performed through Abraham and Sarah was nothing short of the miracle of a resurrection. God took the aging bodies of this faithful couple and gave them the ability to perform that which usually only younger couples are able to accomplish.

---

[10] Hebrews 11:12

The Faith Factor

There is an old song that opens with the line, "Only God can count the apples in a single seed." How marvelous to think that as you hold one small apple seed in your hand, you are literally carrying thousands, if not millions, of future apples! Isaac may have been just one child, yet through him, Abraham and Sarah became parents of an entire nation. At the time this book is being written, the Jewish population stands at 13.3 million. Astounding, isn't it? Even more astounding are the millions of people today who are Abraham's spiritual children. Indeed his offspring are as "numerous as the stars in the sky and as countless as the sand on the seashore." What a remarkable demonstration of God's power!

The second half of the book of Genesis chronicles the lives of Abraham's immediate descendants, known to many as the Patriarchs. From Abraham came Isaac, from Isaac came Jacob, and from Jacob came twelve sons. The twelve sons of Jacob became the foundation for what we know today as the twelve tribes of Israel.

Never underestimate what God can do through you. Stop making excuses for why something cannot possibly happen. Don't live out your life based on your personal limitations. Trust in God and make space for his power to manifest itself in your life.

The Bible tells us that Sarah died at the age of 127.[11] This means she experienced the joy of motherhood for almost four decades after she gave birth at the age of ninety. At a time when most people are prepared to die, she was only beginning to live.

---

[11] Genesis 23:1

The Faith Factor

If someone made you a promise but did not specify when it would be fulfilled, how long do you think you would wait? Two years? Five years? Ten years? Abraham and Sarah waited twenty-five years. And why do you suppose they hung on for so long? I can only imagine that it was because they completely trusted that God could be taken at His word. When God says something, you can believe that it is true.

Jesus gave us a promise that is worth waiting on. In the Gospel of John he said, "I am the resurrection and the life. Those who believe in me, even though they die like everyone else, will live again. They are given eternal life for believing in me and will never perish."[12] This means that as sure as Abraham and Sarah were resurrected to parenthood, we who believe on the Lord Jesus Christ will also experience the power of His resurrection through His gift of eternal life. And that is certainly something worth waiting for.

---

[12] John 11:25-26

chapter

6

Abraham and Isaac: Tested Faith

It was by faith that Abraham offered Isaac as a sacrifice when God was testing him. Abraham, who had received God's promises, was ready to sacrifice his only son, Isaac, even though God had told him, "Isaac is the son through whom your descendants will be counted." Abraham reasoned that if Isaac died, God was able to bring him back to life again. And in a sense, Abraham did receive his son back from the dead.
(Hebrews 11:17-19)

Pop quiz. What do the following have in common?

- Windows operating systems
- Time
- Students
- Patience
- The Emergency Alert System
- Faith

If you guessed, "things that are tested," you are absolutely correct. Being tested is not at all an unusual thing in life. Each of us is tested at every stage of life. For many years as a child, I had to take tests in school. I was tested before being granted a driver's license. I took a comprehensive test for my ordination as a minister. I was given a civics test prior to becoming a U.S. citizen. Until this day, my doctor sends me to the lab several times a year to be tested. Testing is simply inescapable.

As someone who has been both a student and a teacher, I can substantiate that when it comes to testing, it is much more blessed to give than to receive. I hated taking tests when I was in school. I never felt prepared enough. On the day of an exam my blood pressure would rise and I would sweat bullets, especially if the test had anything to do with numbers (I used to think Math was a tool of the devil to make my life miserable). But giving an exam—that's fun! I don't mind putting together a series of questions and watching my students figure out the best way to answer them within a specified period of time. How I wish life was all about giving tests rather than taking them.

There is a perfectly good reason for tests. Would a paratrooper even jump without testing his parachute? Would you swim in a pool that is never tested for pH levels? Would you allow your body to be opened by someone who never passed the Medical Board Exam? Would you give a student a diploma if she failed every midterm and final exam? In each of these cases, the answer is a resounding, "Of course not!" And why so? Because testing, no matter how unpleasant, is the necessary process of sifting the acceptable from the unacceptable. Products that fail tests are rejected, students who fail tests are not permitted to advance, and faith that is not tested is doomed to fail when life's bigger challenges arise.

Abraham's faith was tested. But wait a minute! Wasn't his faith already tested? After all, he did wait twenty-five long years for the promise of God to be fulfilled in his life. Sure he did. And yes, he certainly passed that. However, you and I know that life doesn't just offer one single test. In the course of your life, you will be tested multiple times.

Abraham was tested once and he demonstrated that he had good faith. But as author Jim Collins reminds us, "good is the enemy of great."[1] Abraham's first test was a test of patience and trust. His second one will be a test of commitment and surrender. God was preparing his servant to grow from a man of good faith to a man of great faith.

The stage is set for this new trial. Abraham, now over a century old, finally has the son of promise, Isaac. He loves Isaac dearly. He knows now that God will indeed make him a father of many nations through this young lad. But God was not done with this Patriarch. He had one more test to give Abraham. A test that would determine once and for all the kind of stuff Abraham was made of.

As we look closely at the story of Abraham's ordeal, we can identify four unique qualities of faith that is tested.

I.   Tested faith endures God-given trials.

In the book of Hebrews, the story of Abraham's testing begins with a short, but stunning phrase, "It was by faith that Abraham offered Isaac as a sacrifice when God was testing him."[2] How can this be? How did we get from the joyful birth of Isaac to the offering of Isaac as a sacrifice to God? According to the Genesis account, God determined to test Abraham's obedience. One day, He called out to him and said,

---

[1] Jim Collins, *Good to Great* (Harper Collins Business Publishers, 2001).

[2] Hebrews 11:17a

Abraham.... take your son, your only son—yes Isaac, whom you love so much—and go to the land of Moriah. Sacrifice him there as a burnt offering on one of the mountains, which I will point out to you.[3]

This was a remarkable request, to say the least. God was asking Abraham to give up the very person he patiently waited to see for twenty-five years. God said, "Take your son." It would have been so much easier if God asked for a goat, or a hundred silver coins, or even a dozen of his servants. The Lord didn't ask for any of these. He asked for the son whom Abraham loved so much. Could we love something or someone so much that it actually gets in the way of our primary call to love God supremely? Too often, we are enamored by God's gifts that we lose sight of the preeminence of the Giver of such great gifts.

Furthermore, God was not simply asking Abraham to instruct Isaac to perform some unusual chore. Instead, God was asking him to surrender Isaac back. It didn't make sense. Why would God give Abraham a son, only to ask for the son back? How else would God make Abraham a father of many nations? Would Abraham have to wait another twenty-five years to have another son? This would have been just too much for any of us to face. But remember, Abraham was no ordinary figure of history. God was getting ready to give him much, and to whom much is given, much is required. It was important to determine that Abraham was prepared to hold such an important place in Biblical history.

There is a powerful scene in the film, *Troy*, where a young boy helps Achilles prepare to fight a gigantic warrior. The boy said, "The Thessalyian, he's the biggest man I've seen; I

---

[3] Genesis 22:1-2

wouldn't want to fight him." Achilles then looks at the boy and says, "And that is why your name shall never be remembered." True enough, the only people worth remembering are those who endure great moments of trials and testing. If Abraham was to take his place in history, he needed more than good faith; he needed to have great faith.

God was willing to risk testing Abraham because the Lord never asks of us what He Himself is not willing to provide. He asked Abraham for a great thing, but as we will soon see, He will help provide Abraham with what is needed to pass the test.

II.   Tested faith surrenders to God-given commands.

Surrender is such a hard thing to do. It means giving up control over something and putting it in the rule of another. I am sure that every soldier who has ever surrendered did so with much hesitation. Surrendering makes you vulnerable. You don't know what will happen next nor can you do much about it. In effect, surrender requires faith.

Sometimes you have to decide whether surrendering is ultimately better than not surrendering. With regard to God's will, each of us must choose whether to submit to it or continue to pursue our own. Be aware that the outcome of either choice is often drastically different. Abraham could have chosen to ignore God's command to sacrifice Isaac. If he did, there is no telling what would have happened. However one thing is certain, he would not have been the father of a great nation.

Fortunately, it did not come to that. The Bible says, "Abraham, who had received God's promises, was ready to sacrifice his only son, Isaac."[4] He was ready to sacrifice his only son. That line speaks volumes about the level of Abraham's faith. I must confess that even I might not be at that level. I'm not sure that I am ready to surrender any of my children. Perhaps you are struggling with giving up something to the Lord today. Be assured that you are not alone in the struggle. Great men and women of faith have all undergone such circumstances. Just remember that it is all a test. Do you love God supremely? Or, is something (or someone) getting in the way of full commitment to Him?

Look at how ready Abraham was to obey the Lord:

> The next morning Abraham got up early. He saddled his donkey and took two of his servants with him, along with his son Isaac. Then he chopped wood to build a fire for a burnt offering and set out for the place where God had told him to go. On the third day of the journey, Abraham saw the place in the distance. "Stay here with the donkey," Abraham told the young men. "The boy and I will travel a little farther. We will worship there, and then we will come right back."[5]

God gave Abraham a command and Abraham obeyed the very next morning. What an obedience reflex! No sign of resistance, no attempt to rationalize. Just simple and full obedience to the God he had come to trust fully. He reached a point of no return. He was fully surrendered to God, and now everything was in the Lord's hands.

Abraham's faith is further demonstrated when he said to his servants, "The boy and I will travel a little farther....we will worship there, and then we will come right back." He knew that

---

[4] Hebrews 11:17b
[5] Genesis 22:3-5

God commanded him to sacrifice Isaac, yet he did not say "I will come back." Instead he said, *"We* will come back." This means that Abraham had so much faith in the power of God that he had no problem believing that even if Isaac was to be sacrificed, the Lord would have the power to raise him back to life. After all, he had surrendered all control to God, and now everything rested in God's hands.

III.   Tested faith relies on God-given promises.

Abraham's faith was not mindless belief. It's not like he opened the newspaper, checked his horoscope, and read, "Today will be the perfect day to sacrifice your offspring." Then off he went to sacrifice Isaac. That would be ludicrous. Yet surprisingly, I know people who actually make decisions that way. But that is not Bible faith. As the Hebrew author wrote, "Even though God had told him, 'Isaac is the son through whom your descendants will be counted.' Abraham reasoned that if Isaac died, God was able to bring him back to life again."[6] Abraham's faith was based on reason, not superstition. He assessed the trustworthiness of God, as well as his power, and concluded that the Lord could be trusted even for this. The Lord had been faithful to fulfill His promises in the past so why would He cease to be faithful now? To Abraham, it was all too logical.

As the story goes, Abraham and Isaac took some wood and went up the mountain of sacrifice. Isaac noticed that they had the wood but did not have a lamb, the typical sacrificial animal. "Where is the lamb," he asked. Abraham replied, "God

---

[6] Hebrews 11:18-19

will provide a lamb, my son."[7] Did Abraham have proof of that? Did he actually see a lamb beforehand? No. But he had faith that God would provide. In the Hebrew language, Abraham declared, *Elohim Yirehlo*, which literally means "the Almighty God will provide for himself."

When they reached the top of the mountain, Abraham prepared the wood on the altar, laid Isaac over it, pulled out a knife, and proceeded to sacrifice his boy when an angel interrupted him. "Abraham, Abraham," the angel said, "Lay down the knife....do not hurt the boy in any way, for now I know that you truly fear the Lord....you have not withheld even your beloved son from me."[8] Abraham did it! He proved that he loved God supremely to the point of obeying a command that was utterly difficult to swallow. And with this one act, he will forever be remembered a man of tested faith.

IV.   Tested faith receives God-given blessings.

A person who passes a test is rewarded accordingly. Students who pass get their diploma, a driver-to-be gets his license, and a Bar examinee gets to practice law. As for Abraham, he got his son back. The Bible says, "And in a sense, Abraham did receive his son back from the dead."[9] Isaac experienced a unique kind of resurrection because, although he was as good as dead, he was given back his life.

At the same time, Abraham was still able to give God an offering of sacrifice. For when he looked up, he saw a ram caught by its horns in a bush. Where did this ram come from?

---

[7] Genesis 22:8
[8] Genesis 22:11-12
[9] Hebrews 11:19b

THE FAITH FACTOR

From God, of course. Don't you remember? The Almighty God would provide it for Himself. Abraham took the ram and sacrificed it on the altar in place of his son. He then named the place *Yahweh Yir-eh*,[10] meaning "The Lord will provide."[11] Indeed, whenever we face a great need, the Lord will see to it that it will be provided.

Abraham was blessed with the return of his son and with the provision of a ram. Even more, he was blessed with a reassurance of God's original promise:

> Then the angel of the Lord called again to Abraham from heaven, "This is what the Lord says: Because you have obeyed me and have not withheld even your beloved son, I swear by my own self that I will bless you richly. I will multiply your descendants into countless millions, like the stars of the sky and the sand on the seashore. They will conquer their enemies, and through your descendants, all the nations of the earth will be blessed—all because you have obeyed me.[12]

What does this story teach us? Let me suggest four important lessons that we can learn. First of all, we must be willing to endure each test that God gives. It may seem easier to quit and never take the test. But then, no reward will wait for you if you do. Second, we must trust God even when things don't make sense. We are not capable of understanding how the great mind of God works but we can trust that He is always wise in His ways. Third, we must prioritize God's will over our own. You are free to follow your will, but if you do, do not call

---

[10] Often mispronounced "Jehovah Jireh."
[11] Genesis 22:14
[12] Genesis 22:15-18

yourself a person of faith. A man or woman of faith is fully surrendered to the will of the Lord. And fourth, we must not let anything get in the way of our devotion to God. The greatest commandment is to love God above all. It is not because God is so needy of our love. There is perfect love and harmony among the members of the Trinity. The command to love God above all is designed to help us live out the fullness of what we were created to be—children of God who enjoy the benefits of having fellowship with Him. Anything that gets in the way of our devotion to God diminishes our sense of truth, worth, and purpose.

Have you surrendered your all to God? What is keeping you from giving up that one last thing that is so difficult to let go? I challenge you to trust in God and let Him be proven to be Yahweh Yireh, the Lord who will indeed provided for those whose faith is tried, tested, and proven.

chapter

7

Isaac, Jacob, and Joseph: Enduring Faith

It was by faith that Isaac blessed his two sons, Jacob and Esau. He had confidence in what God was going to do in the future. It was by faith that Jacob, when he was old and dying, blessed each of Joseph's sons and bowed in worship as he leaned on his staff. And it was by faith that Joseph, when he was about to die, confidently spoke of God's bringing the people of Israel out of Egypt. He was so sure of it that he commanded them to carry his bones with them when they left!
(Hebrews 11:20-22)

Dr. James Dobson is one of the most influential Christian leaders in America today. The founder of Focus on the Family has such a following that when he calls for people to contact their representatives to voice concerns about national issues, Congress is literally inundated with millions of phone calls, letters, and emails all in a single day! And to what does Dr. Dobson attribute such influence? To his father, James Dobson Sr. Your see, the senior Dobson was a man who lived out his faith with such integrity that it affected not only his son but also those who, in turn, are inspired by him. Engraved on the tomb of James Dobson, Sr. are two simple, yet very powerful words—"He

Prayed." And because of his legacy of prayer and faith, not only is his son a man of faith, but so are millions of God-fearing Americans. Mr. Dobson had a faith that endures.

In the previous chapters, we learned about Abraham and what a man of faith he truly was. Yet the most powerful aspect of his life was not simply that he believed, but that he was able to pass on the faith to his child, who in turn passed it on to his. In fact, the Bible refers to Abraham as "the father of all who believe,"[1] even to this very day. Subsequently, Abraham and his descendants—Isaac, Jacob, and Joseph—are known as the Patriarchs (i.e., Fathers) of the Judeo-Christian tradition.

When we stop to consider who Isaac, Jacob, and Joseph were, there could not have been a more different bunch. These were three generations of faithful men whose claims to fame were each unique to themselves. Isaac was the son of a famous father as well as the father of a famous son. In a sense, he was famous for being famous. Sort of the way anyone today bearing the name Kennedy or Rockefeller automatically becomes a person of interest, whether or not they actually do something noteworthy. Isaac did not necessarily accomplish great feats, nor was he particularly a spiritual giant. He was, however, trustworthy to pass on the faith of his father to his children. Isaac teaches us that being faithful with the gifts of God is in itself an admirable quality. In a world that celebrates high achievers, perhaps we ought to take time to also acknowledge those who simply do what they do with little desire to draw attention to themselves.

Jacob, on the other hand, was quite famous—or better yet, notorious—for a many number of things. He was primarily

---

[1] Romans 4:16

known for his craftiness. In his early years he used this ability to take away his brother's birthright, and later on steal the same brother's blessing. He went on to wrestle with God himself in an effort to obtain ultimate favor with the Lord. Jacob teaches us that even those who begin life with questionable attributes and behaviors are not beyond the reach of God's grace to be transformed and used for his greater glory.

And then there's Joseph. Could there have been a more honorable man in the Old Testament? At a very young age, Joseph was already famous for being righteous. Ironically, his integrity often led to a life of numerous trials reminiscent of a roller-coaster ride. Yet, Joseph remained faithful to his God until the very end.

I'd like us to think of Isaac, Jacob, and Joseph as Abraham's teammates in a four-man relay. As the baton of faith is passed on from one person to another, each runner imparts a timeless lesson about faith and the blessings of God.

I.   Isaac's faith reveals the true source of blessings.

The author of Hebrews wrote, "It was by faith that Isaac blessed his two sons, Jacob and Esau."[2] This verse refers to the time Isaac was to pass on the covenant blessing shortly before his death. This event, recorded in Genesis 27, was supposed to take place with practically no controversy, but what unfolds is a story worthy of a script for an evening soap opera.

Isaac was blessed with twin boys, Esau and Jacob. It became clear early on that Isaac favored Esau, while his wife, Rebekah, favored Jacob. The boys were polar opposites. Esau

---

[2] Hebrews 11:20a

was a rugged hunter, presumably with a well-built physique, complete with reddish skin and a lot of body hair. He was so hairy at birth that the Bible says, "one would think he was wearing a piece of clothing."[3] Jacob, on the other hand, was your typical ancient mama's boy, one who preferred to stay at home and help with domestic chores.

Because Esau was the firstborn, the blessing of Isaac was rightfully his. However, when the time for the giving of the blessing came, Jacob stole the blessing by pretending to be Esau. How did he pull this off? Why, with the help of his mother, of course.

On the day of blessing, Isaac instructed Esau to hunt for wild game, prepare a meal out of it, and serve it to his father. While Esau went out to hunt, Rebekah prepared a meal of wild game, wrapped Jacob's neck and arms in goatskin, and told the young lad to take the meal to his father. Isaac's eyes were very weak, so he did not recognize Jacob when he entered. He asked, "Who is it—Esau or Jacob?"[4] Jacob lied and replied, "It's Esau." Unconvinced, Isaac asked his son to come closer and upon feeling Jacob's artificially hairy arms, he wondered, "The voice is Jacob's, but the hands are Esau's." In the end, trusting his hands and not his ears, Isaac pronounced the covenant blessing to Jacob, instead of Esau. He passed the blessing to the wrong son! Or did he?

Even if it appeared as though Isaac was deceived into blessing the wrong child, it eventually becomes clear that the blessing of the second child, Jacob, was well within the realm of God's eternal purpose. At the time of their birth, the Lord said to

---

[3] Genesis 25:25
[4] Genesis 27:18

THE FAITH FACTOR

Rebekah, "The sons in your womb will become two rival nations. One nation will be stronger than the other; the descendants of your older son will serve the descendants of your younger son."[5] While the natural order of things dictated that Esau was the rightful heir of the blessing, God in His sovereignty chose otherwise.

Do you ever feel that God cannot bless you or use you because you're not the "right" person? Learn the lesson of Jacob. The blessings of the Lord are not given because it is our right to receive it but because it is God's will to give it.

The Hebrew author goes on to say, "He (Isaac) had confidence in what God was going to do in the future."[6] What happened in the future? What happed was that God truly blessed Jacob. But he overrode Jacob's stolen inheritance by blessing Jacob through a direct confrontation.

After he stole his brother's blessing, Jacob fled his brother's wrath and settled in Haran, his mother's homeland. There, he got married and had many children. In time, Jacob decided to return home and face his brother once again.

In Genesis 32, the eve of the dreaded reunion with his brother, Jacob wrestled with a "man of God."[7] After wrestling all night, the man decided to depart but Jacob would not let him go, insisting, "I will not let you go unless you bless me."[8] So the man asked, "What is your name?" Now remember, the last time he was asked this question, Jacob lied saying, "I am Esau." But this time, he was standing before God Himself and as such, he

---

[5] Genesis 25:23
[6] Hebrews 11:20b
[7] This is believed to be a theophany, an Old Testament appearance of Christ.
[8] Genesis 27:26

could no longer lie. He now replied, possibly with a tone of surrender, "Jacob." The name Jacob means *deceiver*. No wonder it was difficult to admit who he was. Who wants to go around announcing to everyone, "Hello, my name is Deceiver"? But confession of self was exactly what Jacob needed. God cannot bless us unless we are first willing to acknowledge who we truly are before Him, no matter how painful or shameful that revelation might be.

Once Jacob came clean before the Lord, God spoke a new covenant that would change his life forever. God said, "Your name will no longer be Jacob....it is now Israel, because you have struggled with both God and men and have won."[9] Imagine that! Jacob would no longer have to bear the name Deceiver. He was now Israel,[10] the one who struggled with God and won. The covenant blessing was now and forever his, not because he stole it, but because God gave it to him.

Do you have confidence in God for the future? Isaac may have felt awful about giving the blessing to the "wrong" son, but by faith, he chose to trust that in the long run, this was indeed part of God's will. Perhaps it is time for you to stop stealing blessings that don't belong to you and instead trust that through your times of struggle and frustration, the blessing of God awaits you if you only believe. After all, He alone is the source of all true blessings.

---

[9] Genesis 32:28

[10] Some scholars suggest that the name Israel could also mean "Prince of God."

THE FAITH FACTOR

II. Jacob's faith reveals the true provision for blessings.

Many things transpired from the time God gave Jacob the name Israel. Perhaps the most memorable was the episode of losing and finding his favorite son. Jacob had twelve sons but he especially favored Joseph. This aroused the jealousy of the other brothers. One day, they sold Joseph to slave-traders. To cover their tracks, they told their father that a lion ate Joseph. Jacob was crushed. Unbeknownst to him, Joseph embarked on a journey to Egypt that was nothing short of miraculous.

The adventures of Joseph are recorded in Genesis 39-45. Here is what happened in a nutshell. Upon reaching Egypt, Joseph was sold as a slave to a man named Potiphar. He was such a great help that Potiphar gave him charge over the entire household. Unfortunately, Potiphar's wife tried to seduce Joseph, and when Joseph refused her advances, she falsely accused him of rape and had him imprisoned. While in prison, Joseph met Pharaoh's cupbearer who was very impressed that Joseph was able to interpret dreams. The cupbearer was eventually set free and he promised to appeal Joseph's case to Pharaoh. Unfortunately, the cupbearer forgot his promise.

Two years later, Pharaoh had a terrible dream that no one was able to interpret. His cupbearer, remembering his time in prison, told Pharaoh about Joseph, who in turn successfully interpreted the dream. Pharaoh was so impressed that he appointed Joseph to be second-in-command over the entire land of Egypt. Through his great success, Joseph was able to reconnect with his family and had them come to live with him in Egypt. Finally, after many years of trials and testing, Jacob and Joseph were together once again. When they last met, Joseph was a seventeen-year-old lad. But now there he was in his late thirties, no longer a slave but an Egyptian ruler blessed with a wife and two boys, Manasseh and Ephraim.[11]

Now regarding Jacob's testimony, it is written, "It was by faith that Jacob, when he was old and dying, blessed each of Joseph's sons and bowed in worship as he leaned on his staff."[12] This refers to the event recorded in Genesis 48. As Abraham blessed Isaac, and as Isaac blessed Jacob, the time had come for Jacob to bless Joseph and his sons.   Mannaseh and Ephraim were brought to Jacob to be blessed. Then, in true soap-operatic fashion, an unusual thing happened. According to the Genesis account,

> Joseph took the boys from their grandfather's knees, and he bowed low to him. Then he positioned the boys so Ephraim was at Jacob's left hand and Manasseh was at his right hand. But Jacob crossed his arms as he reached out to lay his hands on the boys' heads. So his right hand was on the head of Ephraim, the younger boy, and his left hand was on the head of Mannaseh, the older.[13]

Once again, the "wrong" boy was blessed. Thinking that Jacob was simply confused by his partial blindness, Joseph tried to correct his father by placing the right hand over the older child. Jacob, however, insisted that he knew exactly what he was doing.

What I find most intriguing was the way Jacob blessed his grandchildren by crossing his arms over them. In a sense, this form of blessing was a type of an even more important cross, the one on which the Messiah would be crucified for the sins of the world. As Ephraim and Mannaseh were blessed under the

---

[11] Genesis 41:50-52
[12] Hebrews 11:21
[13] Genesis 48:12-14

shadow of a cross, so too are all who put their faith in Christ our Savior. The death of Jesus Christ is the ultimate provision for eternal blessings. Such a reward does not come from our rights but by God's grace, which is His unmerited favor upon those who believe. Indeed, we are saved by grace through faith.

III.   Joseph's faith reveals the true value of blessings.

After the death of Jacob, Joseph continued to rule in Egypt until he was 110 years old. I'm reminded of the words of Paul when he wrote,

> Children, obey your parents because you belong to the Lord, for this is the right thing to do. "Honor you father and mother." This is the first of the Ten Commandments that ends with a promise. And this is the promise: If you honor your father and mother, "you will live a long life, full of blessing."[14]

Long before the Decalogue was etched in stone, Joseph already exemplified the command to honor his parents. He did so by living in such a way that he brought respect and admiration to their memory. And true to His promise, God blessed Joseph with a long and prosperous life.

Joseph enjoyed temporal blessings that many of us can only dream of. Had he been alive today, he would very well have made the Forbes list of the world's richest people. He was a top official in Egypt, the world's greatest civilization of its day. As a high ranking executive, he would have had access to much wealth, including numerous homes, male and female servants, gold and other currency, and countless other amenities given to

---

[14] Ephesians 6:1-3

royalty. Many today would give an arm and a leg to spend a day in his sandals. Yet ironically, Joseph did not consider the wealth of Egypt his greatest blessing. Instead, the author of Hebrews reminds us,

> And it was by faith that Joseph, when he was about to die, confidently spoke of God's bringing the people of Israel out of Egypt. He was so sure of it that he commanded them to carry his bones with them when they left![15]

Joseph understood that his Egyptian wealth was temporary. Like his great-grandfather, Abraham, he looked forward to the greater blessing of God represented by the Land of Promise. He longed to be wherever God's people were, so that even in death, he ordered his descendants to carry his remains with them on the day God would bring them back to the land of Canaan. For Joseph, the presence of God was a far greater wealth than all that Egypt had to offer. He valued eternal blessings over that which was temporal.

The lives of the Patriarchs teach us so much about true wealth. From them, we learn that God alone is the true source of blessings, that blessings are meant to be guarded faithfully, and that we must know how to pass on these blessings to our children. We are not storehouses of God's favor, rather, we are channels of it through which future generations continue to be blessed.

Although God is certainly more than willing to bless us in this life, the true value of our blessings are realized in the eternity we will spend with our Creator. Are you living only for the riches of this world? Then you are pitifully poor because your

---

[15] Hebrews 11:22

wealth will soon pass away and no more be remembered. But blessed is the one who, like Abraham, Isaac, Jacob, and Joseph, has his eyes fixed on the glory that is Christ and the everlasting riches of His grace.

chapter

8

Moses' Parents: Familial Faith

It was by faith that Moses' parents hid him for three months. They saw that God had given them an unusual child, and they were not afraid of what the king might do.
(Hebrews 11:23)

In the past century, we have witnessed the emergence of many great freedom-fighters. The likes of Gandhi, Martin Luther King Jr., Ninoy Aquino, and Nelson Mandela have made their marks in history and will continue to be remembered for many more years. As fascinating as these men are, I have always been more fascinated with something else. That is, "Who were their parents and what were they like?" Too often, little is said about the fathers and mothers of great men and women. Yet without their parents' guidance and influence, it is doubtful that these notable folks would have achieved the great things that they did.

Long before these 20th century heroes came to the scene, the Hebrew people saw the rise of its great liberator, Moses. Moses is arguably the greatest leader in Old Testament history. But as great as Moses was, have you ever been curious about his parents? Do you even known their names? It seems like the author of Hebrews himself may have forgotten as he simply refers to them as "Moses' parents." But what is not forgotten is what they accomplished. According to Hebrews, "They saw God has given them an unusual child, and they were not afraid of what the king might do."[1] A quick glance at Exodus 1 and 2 will help us understand this verse a little better.

In the previous chapter, we studied the lives of Isaac, Jacob, and Joseph. We learned how God used Joseph to spare the Israelites from famine by relocating them to the land of Egypt. Between the time Joseph died and the period of Moses' birth, about four hundred thirty years[2] had transpired. During this time, the population of Hebrews in Egypt had grown tremendously and for the most part, the Hebrews and the Egyptians coexisted peacefully. However, when a new king came to the throne of Egypt, things drastically changed.

This new king was unaware of the providential circumstances that let the Hebrews live in Egypt. Because of his ignorance he saw the Hebrew presence as a threat to the future welfare of the Egyptian people. Out of fear, he warned his people,

> These Israelites are becoming a threat to us because there are so many of them. We must find a way to put an end to this. If we don't and if war breaks out, they will join our enemies and fight against us. Then they will escape from the country.[3]

---

[1] Hebrews 11:23
[2] Exodus 12:40-41
[3] Exodus 1:9-10

THE FAITH FACTOR

The king's warning caused so much terror in the hearts and minds of the Egyptians that they did horrific things. First, they made the Israelites their slaves forcing them to hard-labor under unbelievably harsh conditions. They did this to break the spirit of the Hebrews and dissuade them from any possibly uprising against the nation of Egypt. Second, the king attempted to control the Hebrew population by doing the unthinkable. He ordered midwives, "When you help the Hebrew women give birth, kill all the boys as soon as they are born. . . . allow only the baby girls to live."[4] He also gave this general order, "Throw all the newborn Israelite boys into the Nile River. . . But you may spare the baby girls."[5] The king rationalized that the absence of Hebrew males would make it impossible for future generations to procreate and increase the population. Such was the condition when Moses' parents, Amram and Jochebed, were blessed with the birth of their son.

In this chapter, we will explore how Amram and Jochebed responded to the king's edict regarding the birth of Moses and extract some important lessons they teach us about faithful parenting.

I. Faithful parents serve as guardians to their children

We read in Hebrews that, "It was by faith that Moses' parents hid him for three months when he was born."[6] Even though the king demanded the death of male babies, Amram and Jochebed guarded baby Moses at the risk of their own lives. Every parent surely understands what they must have felt. After

---

[4] Exodus 1:16
[5] Exodus 1:22
[6] Hebrews 11:23a

all, what father or mother would not be willing to risk his or her own life in order to protect a child from harm?

There are some in the animal kingdom that are able to survive independently from the day they are born. Not so with humans. Babies are born helpless and utterly dependent on another for survival. Leave a newborn child alone to fend for itself and he or she will not be alive much longer. Even after birth, children continue to need parental help in the areas of nurture, guidance, and protection. Yet as noble as it is for a parent to provide for a child's physical needs, it is equally, if not more important, to provide a child with spiritual guidance and protection. Moses' parents proved capable of creating both physical and spiritual safeguards around their newborn son. For three whole months, they kept Moses' birth a secret so that the Egyptians would not find him and throw him into the Nile River.

Can you imagine how difficult it must have been to keep such a thing concealed from the authorities? Jochebed had to nurse Moses in secrecy, keep Moses' cries from being heard, and go about her daily life in the village as if she did not have a newborn son. With such dedicated parents, what does a child have to fear?

Unfortunately, there is much to indicate that parents today may not be doing a good job in quelling the fears of today's children. A group of researchers from John Hopkins University conducted a survey thirty years ago to discover the prevailing fears among grade school children. The top five fears revealed were: 1) animals, 2) being in a dark room, 3) heights, 4) strangers and 5) loud noises. A similar study was conducted recently and the results were astounding. It showed that the top five fears of grades school children today are: 1) divorce, 2) nuclear war, 3) cancer, 4) pollution, and 5) being mugged. It's amazing how much can change in thirty short years!

Could it be that we, the supposed guardians of helpless children, are responsible for actually creating situations wherein kids are made to feel more fearful rather than secure? If our children are to grow up to be confident of who they are as people of value and great worth, then it is incumbent upon us parents to provide a conducive environment for stable growth. Furthermore, if these same children are to become people of faith and committed followers of Jesus, we are equally responsible for instilling these faith values in their lives while they are still young. The fact of the matter is that there are so many negative forces vying for our children's attention and affection these days. As parents, how well are we protecting our children from such dangerous things? Moses' parents clearly did a great job protecting their son from the evil of their day.

II. Faithful parents see God's potential in their children

The Bible says that Amram and Jochebed "saw that God had given them an unusual child."[7] The Exodus account states that when Moses was born, his mother "saw what a beautiful baby he was."[8] There is something special about children. I remember when I first held my son I was completely struck by how magnificent the work of God is. Somehow, a simplistic understanding of how human reproduction works was not sufficient to explain the wonder of a newborn child.

---

[7] Hebrew 11:23b
[8] Exodus 2:2b

THE FAITH FACTOR

I suppose every parent has an innate impulse to let the world know how wonderful his or her child is. Sometimes even well-meaning parents exaggerate their claims while others even engage in a "my-child-is-better-than-your-child" combat with other parents. I once heard a mom say, "My baby started walking at ten months," at which the other mom retorted, "O really? Mine started walking at nine and a half months!" It's all quite amusing, if not a little irritating at times. However, we must understand that there is a big difference between bragging that your child is special and having a child who is truly unique in his or her role in God's unfolding of the drama that is human history. Moses was one such child.

If a parent is a man or woman of faith, he or she is given the ability to see in a child what might otherwise be glossed over as commonplace. A wise parent will capture the essence of a child's God-ordained uniqueness and harness it by encouraging a child to grow in his or her area of giftedness. A faithful parent will do so within the context of committing the child's giftedness as an act of worship and service to God. Take the case of a child named Tommy who was born in Ohio in 1847. When he started going to school at the age of seven, he was considered a nuisance by his teachers because he was always asking questions and seeking clarification on the lectures. The teachers concluded that he was retarded, and after only three months of schooling they recommended that Tommy drop schooling altogether. Tommy's mother, refusing to give up on her child, chose to educate the boy herself. Because of her unwavering commitment to teach him, Tommy grew up to become an inventor. You might be familiar with a few of his inventions which include the light bulb, the phonograph, and the telegraph. Tommy, better known as Thomas Edison, may have been overlooked by his teachers yet he grew up to become a person of prominence because of a parent who saw something special in him.

    I love my parents. As a child, they believed in me even at times when I didn't believe in myself. Growing up, I was an average student. I didn't exhibit extra-ordinary skills in any particular area. I did okay in school. Some years I made the honor roll while other years I didn't. I remember one particular year in high school. The policy in our school required parents to come and pick up our report cards so that teachers would have an opportunity to provide feedback. That year, I literally missed the honor roll by a point or two. Handing the report card to my mom, my teacher commented, "You know Mrs. Miciano, Ed would be a better student if only he tried a little harder." My heart was crushed. I was almost sure my mom would scold me in front of my teacher and friends. Instead my mom did something I totally did not expect. She took the report card from the teacher and said, "You know Mrs. Garcia (not her real name), I've seen the effort Ed puts in his schoolwork and he is quite a hardworking boy." Then looking at the report card, she added, "And I'm very satisfied with the grades he got this year." It's as if a heavy burden was lifted off my shoulders! I don't know if my mom realized what she did that day, but it changed me forever. If my mom was pleased with me and my performance, then I had nothing else to prove to anyone. I can honestly say that that was the day I actually started liking school. Thank God for faithful parents---thank God for parents of faith.

    Do you have a tendency to be overly-critical of your child? Have you been focusing on his or her negative traits while completely ignoring what makes him or her special in the eyes of God. I challenge you to be like Moses' parents. Look into your child's eyes and see that that person is someone unusual—a special person called to do special things.

III. Faithful parents acknowledge God's sovereignty over their children

The edict was clear—all newborn baby boys were to be thrown into the Nile River. Yet Amram and Jochebed knew in their hearts that even though failure to surrender their son would be a violation of Pharaoh's law, allowing their son to be killed was a violation of God's law. In light of this dilemma, the author of Hebrews wrote, "They were not afraid to disobey the king's commands."[9] Indeed, the king of Egypt was to be feared, but the Lord God was to be feared even more.

Imagine the quandary faced by Moses' parents. How can they get away with disobeying the rule of a powerful king? For three months they managed to keep Moses hidden. But who were they kidding? Baby Moses was growing and soon he will be walking about and talking. Surely they could not hide him forever. After much deliberation, Amram and Jochebed decided to release their child and leave his fate in the hands of God. What a heart-breaking decision this must have been! As a father of three, I cannot even begin to imagine what it would be like to be faced with this situation.

According to Exodus 2:3-10, Jochebed placed Moses in a basket and laid the basket along the banks of the Nile River. Moses' sister was instructed to follow the basket as it floated down the river in order to see what would become of their beloved baby. Incredibly, the basket went down to a part of the

---

[9] Hebrews 11:23c

river where Pharaoh's daughter was bathing. When the princess saw the basket and the baby in it, she noticed that it was a Hebrew child (probably based on Moses' appearance, as well as the kind of fabric he was wrapped in).

Moses' sister, having followed the basket to this place, immediately offered the princess to find a person to care for this "abandoned" child. When the princess agreed, Moses' sister called on her own mother to care for the baby. The princess told Jochebed, "Take this child home and nurse him for me. . . .I will pay you for your help."[10] Can you imagine that? Not only did Jochebed get her son back, she even got paid by the princess for doing something most mothers would have done for free!

When Moses was older, Jochebed brought him back to Pharaoh's daughter who adopted him as her own son. It must have saddened Jochebed to give up her son this way. But through the providence of God, she was privileged to raise Moses for many years, and by doing so she was given the awesome opportunity to instill in Moses the faith and the values of God's chosen people.

God proved to Amram and Jochebed that when they learned to surrender everything to God and trust in His gracious sovereignty, He will work things out in ways that will amaze them. I remember a line from a song that says, "Praise His name and see it happen!" People of faith move, not based on knowing how all things work, but on knowing that God knows how to best work all things.

In today's culture, parents have many fears regarding their children's future. We fear the threats of war, disease, drugs, sexual temptation, and other societal ills. Yet despite these

---

[10] Exodus 2:9

dangers, we ought to learn how to trust that God always has our children's best interests in mind. That is why we should teach our children to love and revere the Lord our God.

The idea of raising children in a household of faith is so dear to the heart of God that even the *Shema Yisrael*, the great declaration of God's people, is written within the context of the godly family. Used in daily Jewish prayers, the Shema reads,

> Hear, O Israel! The LORD is our God, the LORD alone. And you must love the LORD your God with all your heart, all your soul, and all your strength. And you must commit yourselves wholeheartedly to these commands I am giving you today. Repeat them again and again to your children. Talk about them when you are at home and when you are away on a journey, when you are lying down and when you are getting up again. Tie them to your hands as a reminder, and wear them on your forehead. Write them on the doorposts of your house and on your gates.[11]

Parents ought to take seriously the stewardship role given to them by God. As faithful stewards, we must commit to raise our children in the ways of God, thereby instilling in them a faith that will guide them all the days of their lives. Amram and Jochebed did this under extraordinary circumstances, and therefore, proved to be people of faith because they trusted God in the midst of very trying times—and they did so for the sake of their beloved child.

---

[11] Deuteronomy 6:4-9

chapter

9

Moses: Independent Faith

It was by faith that Moses, when he grew up, refused to be treated as the son of Pharaoh's daughter. He chose to share the oppression of God's people instead of enjoying the fleeting pleasures of sin. He thought it was better to suffer for the sake of the Messiah than to own the treasures of Egypt, for he was looking ahead to the great reward that God would give him. It was by faith that Moses left the land of Egypt. He was not afraid of the king. Moses kept right on going because he kept his eyes on the one who is invisible. It was by faith that Moses commanded the people of Israel to keep the Passover and to sprinkle blood on the doorposts so that the angel of death would not kill their first born sons.
(Hebrews 11:24-28)

A recent Gallup poll revealed a troubling reality faced by the modern church. At a convention of Southern Baptist Churches, George Gallup reported,

> We find there is very little difference in ethical behavior between churchgoers and those who are not active religiously . . . The levels of lying, cheating, and stealing are remarkably similar in both groups. Eight out of ten Americans consider themselves Christians, yet only about half of them could identify the person who gave the Sermon on the Mount, and

fewer still could recall five of the Ten Commandments. Only two in ten said they were willing to suffer for their faith.

It is a sad day when the behavioral patterns of God's people are indistinguishable from the lifestyles of those who live by purely secular norms. One preacher lamented, "These days the church is getting worldly and the world is getting churchy that it's becoming difficult to tell the difference between the two."

When God elected to raise a chosen people, He made it clear that He expected them to behave in a way that set them apart from the nations of the world. That is why God gave specific commandments to His people. He not only gave moral directives but even dealt with otherwise mundane things such as diet, clothing, and a variety of relational concerns. His purpose was to set His people apart—to make them holy.

The biblical notion of holiness stems from the principle of separation. The Hebrew and Greek words for holiness, *qodesh* and *hagiosune*, both mean "a setting apart." Primarily, believers are set apart in a spiritual sense, but there ought to be a physical manifestation of this separation in order for it to be clearly observed by others. This is the reason why God expects His people to exhibit behavioral qualities that reflect their inner holiness. Merely acting "holy" does not automatically mean one is, but one who is truly holy must, by necessity, act in a way that is consistent with one's spiritual condition. That absence of substantive behavior manifesting holiness has often been referred to as *worldliness*.

There are three ways in which the word *world* is used in Scripture. First, *world* can simply refer to the planet earth. For instance, the Bible says, "His lightning lights up the world."[1] Second, *world* can refer to humanity or the inhabitants of the planet earth. The famous line, "For God so loved the world..."[2] is a prime example of this. Third, *world* can mean the sinful human culture that governs fallen humanity. When John warns us, "Stop loving this evil world and all it offers you, for when you love the world, you show that you do not have the love of the Father in you,"[3] he is not saying that we live in an evil planet. Rather, he is affirming that the unregenerate people in this world live by norms and standards that do not reflect the holy nature of God. The system of a sinful culture is worldly.

Moses was a man who had both a spiritual and a worldly upbringing. In his early years, he was nurtured by his mother, a Hebrew who instilled in Moses a sense of connection with God and His people. Later, he was adopted by Pharaoh's daughter and enjoyed the earthly pleasures of Egyptian royalty. When the time came for him to make a decision as to where his loyalty would lie, he made the difficult but honorable choice to give up the glory of Egypt and live among the people of God. Moses was a man of independent faith. He did not allow the worldliness of Egypt to dictate how he would live. Instead, he lived as a child of the Lord, the God of Israel.

I.   Moses had the faith to refuse what the world had to offer.

By faith, Moses responded to God's call to leave the world and pursue God's promise to his people. He had the faith

---

[1] Psalm 97:4, NIV
[2] John 3:16
[3] 1 John 2:15

to say *no* to the world and say *yes* to God. The independent faith of Moses was marked by a series of refusals of all this world had to offer.

He refused the prestige of Egypt. Moses "refused to be treated as the son of Pharaoh's daughter."[4] He was, as one film title suggests, *Prince of Egypt*. As a member of the Egyptian royal family, Moses would have been educated in the best schools and given the best military training. He had a special place in the royal courts and conceivably may have held a high rank in the Egyptian army. He had an identity that most everyone else could have only dreamed of.

How easy it would have been for Moses to continue living with such esteem. In Egypt, he was somebody special. However, Moses willingly gave up his status in order to gain identity with God. By doing so, he showed us that worldly fame, although it was often coveted, was no match for being known by the One who mattered most.

He refused the pleasures of Egypt. Moses "chose to share the oppression of God's people instead of enjoying the fleeting pleasures of sin."[5] Imagine all the temporal delights that were within Moses' reach. As prince of Egypt, he must have had access to unimaginable worldly pleasures that would have included rich foods, fine wines, plush homes, and luxuries that would dwarf the possessions of even wealthy people today. The Bible further states that he also could have enjoyed sin-based pleasures which may refer to the excessive indulging of sensual appetites.

---

[4] Hebrews 11:24
[5] Hebrews 11:25

The Faith Factor

I truly believe that Jochebed's early influence on her son must have played a role in his decision to refuse the pleasures of Egypt, and instead, share in the plight of the Hebrew people. Moses saw the pleasures of Egypt for what they were, fleeting pleasures that only supplied momentary happiness, but failed to provide true and lasting satisfaction. The Bible says that "godliness with contentment is great gain"[6] and Moses discovered that to be true in his own life. True pleasure, one that lasts forever, is only found in a loving and genuine relationship with the God who created us.

He refused the treasures of Egypt. Moses "thought it was better to suffer for the sake of the Messiah than to own the treasures of Egypt, for he was looking ahead to the great reward that God would give him."[7] What kind of person would willingly give up actual, tangible wealth for something not yet seen? Only a person with the eyes of faith.

There was an incident in the life of Moses where he killed an Egyptian who was beating on a Hebrew slave. When word of this got to Pharaoh, he gave orders to have Moses arrested and killed.[8] So Moses fled to the land of Midian where he worked as a shepherd for forty years. In ancient times, there could not have been two more dissimilar jobs as a prince and a shepherd. A prince was wealthy and highly esteemed. A shepherd, on the other hand, was a lowly laborer with very little clout in society. In some cultures, shepherds were not even permitted to give legal testimonies in court because their words were not considered credible.

---

[6] 1 Timothy 6:6, NIV
[7] Hebrews 11:26
[8] Exodus 2:11-15

The Faith Factor

When the Bible says that Moses gave up the treasures of Egypt, this was no small feat. Imagine someone like Bill Gates or the king of Saudi Arabia renouncing their worldly riches and working as janitors in some third world country. That's exactly what Moses did. But in giving up the wealth of the world, he received a much greater treasure. He forsook earthly wealth for heavenly wealth—the "reward of God" that awaits all who put their faith in the Lord.

He refused the inheritance of Egypt. Fearing God more than the king, Moses left the land of Egypt. He "kept right on going because he kept his eyes on the one who is invisible."[9] Although Moses was not directly next in line to become king, he was certainly within the general line of succession. If for any reason Pharaoh's sons were unable to ascend to their father's throne, Moses had a fairly good chance of becoming king himself. And even if he never actually became a king, he would nonetheless be the recipient of an unimaginable inheritance as a member of the royal family. Many of us today dream of leaving behind a substantial financial inheritance for our children so that they would be spared from some of the hardships we face in life. Moses already had such an inheritance in his hands, yet he willingly gave it up.

Once Moses gave up the treasures and inheritance of Egypt, he did not look back. Instead, he "kept his eyes on the one who is invisible." Quite oxymoronic, isn't it? How can one look at someone who is invisible? This is only possible when we learn how to look through the eyes of faith. In the opening line of Hebrews 11, we learned that faith is "the evidence of things

---

[9] Hebrews 11:27

we cannot yet see."[10] Faith is lived out in the physical realm but operates in the spiritual realm. That is why it is so difficult for people without faith to comprehend the way we live. Many of our choices and decisions do not make sense when assessed by worldly standards. The decision of Moses to refuse the riches of Egypt must have boggled the minds of the Egyptians, and perhaps, even some of the Hebrews of that day.

He refused the fate of Egypt. The Bible reminds us that "it was by faith that Moses commanded the people of Israel to keep the Passover and to sprinkle blood on the doorposts, so that the angel of death would not kill their firstborn sons."[11] It might be helpful to rewind the story a little bit in order to understand what this means.

Moses, now a shepherd in Midian, encountered God in the famous "burning bush" experience recorded in Exodus 3 and 4. He was told by God to return to Pharaoh and demand the release of the Hebrew people. When Moses did as God commanded, demanding Pharaoh to "let my people go," the king hardened his heart and refused to release the Israelites. Because of this, God unleashed a series of plagues[12] that inflicted the people of Egypt. The last of these ten plagues was a visit from the "angel of death" over all the firstborn of the land. The only way to be spared from this curse was to take the blood of a sacrificial animal and sprinkle it on the doorposts of each home. When death came to the land of Egypt, it inflicted every unprotected home. It would, however, pass over the homes that were protected by the covering of blood (hence the term "Passover").

---

[10] Hebrews 11:1b
[11] Hebrews 11:28
[12] For a complete description of the plagues read Exodus 7-11.

Because of their faithful obedience, the people of Israel were spared from this awful plague. The people of Egypt, on the other hand, suffered a tremendous blow with the loss of all their firstborn children, including the firstborn of their livestock. Such was the fate of Egypt that Moses was spared from. By forsaking all that Egypt had to offer, Moses did not share in Egypt's punishment.

A similar scenario confronts all of us today. We have before us everything that the world has to offer. The sinful things of this world, both treasures and pleasures, are undoubtedly enjoyable. Unfortunately, they are all fleeting. At the end of every sinful experience is death and destruction. The only escape is to be covered by the blood of Jesus, the sacrificial Lamb of God. Just as Moses was spared from the fate of Egypt, we who believe in the Lord Jesus Christ will also be spared from the deadly consequences of sin.

II.   The believer's response to worldliness

The "Egypt" of our day is the modern world. The temptations we face in this world are just as real as the ones faced by Moses. Like Moses, we are called to live out an independent faith, one that is not controlled by the sinful forces of this world. In his first epistle, the Apostle John warns,

> Stop loving this evil world and all that it offers you, for when you love the world, you show that you do not have the love of the Father in you. For the world offers only the lust for physical pleasure, the lust for everything we see, and pride in our possessions. They are not from the Father. They are from this evil world. And this world is fading away, along with

everything it craves. But if you do the will of God, you will live forever.[13]

Furthermore, the Apostle Paul offers a similar admonition when he wrote,

> Don't copy the behavior and customs of this world, but let God transform you into a new person by changing the way you think. Then you will know what God wants you to do, and you will know how good and pleasing and perfect his will really is.[14]

Have you truly learned to give up the counterfeit riches of this world for the eternal riches of God? Has the will of God so captured your thinking that you no longer pattern your behavior by the standards of this world? Keep in mind that although the wealth of this world is alluring, it always comes with strings attached.

In the ancient kingdom of Siam, the monarch had an unusual way of ruining a person who was unwise enough to cause him anger or grief. The king would present such a person with the gift of an elephant. What a nice gesture! Or is it? In reality, the average citizen, who would never dare refuse a gift from the king, could not afford to maintain such a "useless" gift. In time, the elephant would literally eat all of a person's wealth, leading him or her to utter bankruptcy. What originally appeared to be a blessing was actually a curse.

The things of this world can likewise appear to be a blessing. Drawn to its charm, we make every effort to buy bigger homes and drive fancier cars. We consume the world's

---

[13] 1 John 2:15-17
[14] Romans 12:2

goods as one with avaricious appetites. Before we know it, such pleasures rob us of our spiritual wealth and leave us morally bankrupt. Alas, the elephants of the world have eaten their way into our lives until we have nothing left that is of worth!

If we live by faith, we will readily give up the ephemeral pleasures of this world and keep our eyes on the eternal rewards of God in His kingdom.

chapter

10

The People of Israel (Part I): Courageous Faith

It was by faith that the people of Israel went right through the Red Sea as though they were on dry ground. But when the Egyptians followed, they were all drowned.
(Hebrews 11:29)

Do you believe in miracles? According to a survey conducted by the Princeton Religion Research Center, eighty-two percent of people believe that even today miracles are performed by the power of God. That's a remarkably large number given the fact that Western culture appears to be more secular than ever before.

It would be interesting to know how the respondents of the survey defined the word *miracle*. I'm afraid that, too often, we describe most everything as miraculous that the term ceases to be as powerful as it is meant to be. Sometimes we find a desirable parking spot in our favorite mall and exclaim, "It's a miracle!" We make it sound as if all the powers of heaven were harnessed to ensure that you would have the best place to park in order to do your holiday shopping. When we describe events like these as miraculous, we actually end up trivializing the intended impact of a true miracle.

In the New Testament, one of the most common terms for miracle is the word *dunamis*. It literally means "power" and is used to describe any number of phenomena that is ascribed to a supernatural cause. According to Webster's dictionary, a miracle is "an event or effect that apparently contradicts known scientific laws and is, hence, thought to be due to supernatural cause, especially an act of God."

As I see it, a miracle is a supernatural manifestation of divine power in the natural world. Although anybody can be a potential recipient of a miracle, the Bible seems to indicate that most miracles take place as a response to faith, specifically, faith in the ability of God to perform something extraordinary. Whereas many people insist on seeing something miraculous before they believe, Scripture demonstrates that miracles come after one chooses to believe. St. Augustine stated it this way, "Faith is to believe what we do not see; the reward of this faith is to see what we believe."

Up until now, we have been exploring the faith of individual believers in the Old Testament. Here we will look into the faith of an entire nation—the people of Israel. Specifically, we will see how the collective faith of the Israelites teaches us to have courageous faith.

In the previous chapter, we studied how, by faith, Moses refused the worldly splendor of Egypt. Since then, several events had transpired by the time we get to the story we are about to examine. We know that Moses was called by God to deliver the Israelites from Egyptian bondage. After a tense confrontation with Pharaoh that included the curse of the 10 plagues, the people of Israel were eventually released. However, Pharaoh regretted his decision and ordered his army to pursue the Israelites in the desert in order to reclaim them as Egyptian slaves. When we read the beginning of Exodus 14, the people of God are caught between a rock and a hard place. In front of them was the massive Red Sea and behind them was the Egyptian army. They were stuck with apparently no good alternative. They were in an impossible situation and needed help—they needed a miracle! The rest of Exodus 14, coupled with Hebrews 11:29, reveals three facts about how God works in light of such critical moments.

I. God operates best under extremely desperate circumstances

You don't need a miracle unless you are in a crisis, and the people of Israel were in one. Technically, as crisis is a situation in which you have lost all ability to cope. If, for instance, you get a letter from the IRS stating that you still owe $10,000 in back taxes, is that a crisis? If you are billionaire, it is not, if you are me, it is.

The Israelites had no human ability to cope with their situation. There was no way they could all cross the Red Sea in front of them and neither could they possibly defeat the superior army of Egypt. Fortunately, God never sweats over a crisis. In fact, He thrives in it.

The Hebrew writer wrote, "It was by faith that the people of Israel went right through the Red Sea. . ."[1] How did they manage this? By faith, of course. According to Exodus 14:15-

---

[1] Hebrews 11:29a

20, there are three things we must remember when we are in a similar dilemma. First of all, God expects us to act in faith. Rather than performing the miracle immediately, the Lord said to Moses,

> Why are you crying out to me? Tell the people to get moving! Use your shepherd's staff—hold it out over the water, and a path will open up before you through the sea. Then all the people of Israel will walk through on dry ground.[2]

Do you realize what God was asking Moses to do? He was telling Moses to take the first step. God is always prepared to do something miraculous, but often He simply waits for us to make a move—to step out in faith.

Secondly, God can use our enemies to reveal His glory. Rather than eliminate the armies of Egypt, God allowed them to pursue the Israelites. He did this to leave no doubt that the ensuing miracle was a result of His power and that He alone was worthy of the glory. The Lord himself said, "The Egyptians will know that I am the Lord when I gain glory through Pharaoh, his chariots, and his horsemen."[3] Too often, we expect God to get rid of our enemies when, in fact, His plan is to reveal His glory to us in the presence of our enemies. Having faith means that we trust that God is able to defend us no matter how powerful our adversaries might be.

Thirdly, God's Spirit will stand between us and our enemy. God led his people out of Egypt by a pillar of cloud that stood in front of people. Now that the Egyptian army was pursuing them, the cloud of God moved from the front and

---

[2] Exodus 14:15-16
[3] Exodus 14:18, NIV.

moved behind the Israelites, thereby creating a hedge of protection between them and the Egyptians. This cloud was as a double-edged sword, in that it "brought darkness to the one side and light to the other side."[4] The same presence of God that dimmed the path of the enemy also shone brightly to light a path for His believing people. If God is on your side, do not ever fear your enemies, for though they may be more powerful than you, they will never be more powerful than your God.

In times of crises, attitude is everything. You can choose to look at your problem and see a mountain impossible to climb, or an opportunity to see the beauty of what lies on the other side. What crisis are you facing today? Are you able to trust that God is fully aware and in control of that which you are worried about?

II.   God has the power to defy reason

God doesn't always make sense to us because His ways are not our ways.[5] If the Red Sea crisis was under my jurisdiction, I would simply zap the Egyptian army into oblivion and let the Israelites go on their merry way into the Promised Land. Problem solved, case closed. Somehow God had another thing in mind. The Bible says that the Israelites crossed the Red Sea "as though they were on dry ground."[6] In the Exodus account it reads,

> Then Moses raised his hand over the sea, and the LORD opened up a path through the water with a strong east wind. The wind blew all that night, turning the seabed into dry land. So the

---

[4] Exodus 14:20, NIV.
[5] Isaiah 55:8
[6] Hebrews 11:29b, NIV

people of Israel walked through the sea on dry ground, with walls of water on each side![7]

God is so powerful that He can use methods that defy our understanding. He has power over nature, which was evident in this story. Amazingly, the Red Sea parted so that there was a wall of water on one side and another wall on the other, leaving the path in the middle completely dry. God created a path where there was previously no path at all. As people of faith, we must remember that our God is not limited by human frailty. What is impossible for us is not impossible with Him. Faith works in spite of our ability to make sense of what God is asking us to believe.

Furthermore, God not only defies human reason but He also leads us to experience such defiance first hand. In the case of the Israelites, the Lord expected them to actually cross the path of the Red Sea, not simply be in awe that the sea actually parted. This was such a massive endeavor, considering that as much as two million Israelites crossed this miraculous land bridge. The Bible says that God held back the waters "all that night" as it would have taken that long for all of His people to cross safely to the other side.

I meet many people who fail to trust God because they don't fully understand him. Yet these same people go about their daily lives trusting in things they do not fully understand. I don't know exactly how a fax machine transmits an exact copy of a document across ten thousand miles of ocean, but that doesn't stop me from using it. Every day, millions of people don't understand the laws of aerodynamics enough to know how a two

---

[7] Exodus 14:21-22

hundred ton metal tube can defy gravity and float in the air, but that doesn't stop them from strapping themselves in airplanes. Every day we have enough faith to trust in things we don't understand. Why then is it so difficult to trust in God who has proven Himself to be trustworthy for as long as we can recall.

Do you find it difficult to believe God can rescue you from crisis because nothing seems to make sense? Perhaps you have depended on people before, only to be disappointed by your misplaced trust. When we get hurt by others, especially those near and dear to us, it is easy to take the stance of a recluse, unwilling to trust anyone else because our painful experience makes it senseless to do so. I want you to know that God is not a man that He will fail you in your time of need. I encourage you to believe that in times of crisis, trusting in God is the only thing that makes sense.

III. God gives victory to those who have the courage to believe

God rewards courageous faith. The Bible says that "when the Egyptians followed, they were all drowned."[8] A person of faith learns very quickly that when you are on God's side, your enemies become God's enemies. That means that you are far more capable of dealing with your crisis than you think.

Moses learned that although a stick is just a stick, a stick in the hands of a man of faith is a powerful weapon even against the greatest army in the world. In the miraculous account of Exodus 14:23, the Egyptian army pursued the Israelites as they crossed the Red Sea. But as the last of them crossed over, the

---

[8] Hebrews 11:29c

Lord commanded Moses to once again stretch his hand over the sea. With this, the waters returned to the ground. Seeing this, the Egyptians cried out, "Let's get out of here! . . . The LORD is fighting for Israel against us!"[9] The army of Egypt turned back but it was too late. Soon the water flowed back and the entire army was drowned. None of Israel's enemies survived.

When our enemies are close, God is even closer. There is no force on earth that can defeat us when we are under God's protection. Jesus said, "Do not be afraid of those who kill the body but cannot kill the soul."[10] Furthermore, those who put their trust in God will outlive their enemies and will savor the taste of victory. The people of Israel learned an important lesson the day they crossed the Red Sea. The Bible says, "When the people of Israel saw the mighty power that the Lord had displayed against the Egyptians, they feared the Lord and put their faith in him and his servant Moses."[11]

When we were younger, my brother and I enjoyed watching the old Superman TV series starring George Reeves. However, there was one thing that puzzled us. Each episode would open with the familiar words, "Faster than a speeding bullet, more powerful than a locomotive, and able to leap tall buildings in a single bound." This was accompanied by a scene where gangsters fired shots at Superman, but to no avail, because the bullets would simply bounce off his chest. Suddenly, one guy runs out of bullets, so he throws the gun at Superman—and Superman ducks! Why? If the bullets didn't hurt him, why did he dodge the gun? Didn't the man of steel realize that the gun

---

[9] Exodus 14:25
[10] Matthew 10:28, NIV
[11] Exodus 14:31

The Faith Factor

was just as powerless against him as the bullets? So much for the magic of fantasy television.

About two thousand years ago, Jesus died for us and gave us victory over sin and death. And if God has already given us this great victory, why should we worry about anything else that threatens us? Does it feel like your enemies are winning over you? Be strong, take courage, and trust that your enemies can do you no harm because the victory is already yours in Christ Jesus our Lord.

chapter

11

The People of Israel (Part II): Obedient Faith

It was by faith that the people of Israel marched around Jericho seven days, and the walls came crashing down.
(Hebrews 11:30)

September 11, 2001, will forever be etched in the memories of those in my generation. On that tragic morning, we were all glued to our television sets as we watched in horror the fall of New York City's Twin Towers. Earlier that day, commercial airliners were hijacked by terrorists and deliberately crashed into these famous landmarks. Moments later, each of the two towers succumbed to the sweltering heat of the flames and fell to the ground as if they were mere sandcastles kicked by the local bully. It all seemed like a bad disaster movie. After all, how could such a superstructure stand erect one day and be totally demolished the next?

Centuries ago, another superstructure fell to the ground. But unlike the 9/11 tragedy, this was not the work of fiendish terrorists, rather, it was an act of the Almighty God. The story of the fall of Jericho's great wall is a classic children's church tale that continues to yield lessons of faith for believers of all ages. Although the Israelites in the wilderness were notorious for their murmuring and disobedience, every once in a while, they demonstrated a remarkable capacity for faith. The conquest of Jericho under the leadership of Joshua was one such time.

The story is found in the sixth chapter of the book of Joshua. A brief historical review will help us understand the setting of this tale. Forty years transpired between the victory at the Red Sea and the beginning of the conquest of the Promised Land. The generation of Hebrews that escaped Egyptian bondage wandered in the wilderness for forty years, in which time they raised a new generation of Hebrews born during the wilderness experience. Those of the older generation, including Moses, died before having the chance to enter the Promised Land. There were, however, two exceptions, one of whom was a man named Joshua.

Joshua, the son of Nun, was about forty years old when the Hebrews left Egypt. Toward the end of the forty year journey in the wilderness, he was one of twelve spies who were sent to Canaan to scout the land and prepare the Israelites to conquer it. When the spies returned, ten of them gave an unfavorable report citing that the people of Canaan were powerful and their cities were fortified, so that it was doubtful that the Hebrews could overpower them. The other two spies, Joshua and Caleb, gave a very different report. They said, "The land we explored is a wonderful land! . . . And if the Lord is pleased with us, He will bring us safely into that land and give it to us."[1] God was clearly pleased with this demonstration of

---

[1] Numbers 14:7-8

faith, and Joshua was blessed by being selected as the successor of Moses. In fact, it was he, not Moses, who was chosen to lead the people into the Promised Land.

There was one thing that stood between the Israelites and their land of promise—the fortified city of Jericho. Past the Jordan River, Jericho was the fortress city that guarded all the paths leading to the interior of Canaan. The city itself was surrounded by a thick double wall about three miles in circumference. The outer wall was six feet thick and the inner wall was twelve feet thick, with a space of fifteen feet between walls. The wall was so wide that some scholars suggest chariots once raced around the top of the structure. Beyond its physical grandeur, Jericho had a spiritual significance in that it was the most significant obstacle that kept the Israelites from realizing the fulfillment of God's promise.

We all face spiritual Jerichos at some point in our lives. It is that which stands between you and God's promise. Perhaps your Jericho appears so intimidating that you wonder if there is any possible way to conquer it. It is simply too wide to get around and too high to get over. It can be an incurable disease, or a financial predicament, or even internal anguish that is so powerful that you are tempted to call it quits. I encourage you to hang in there and learn the lesson of how to exercise obedient faith in the face of such gigantic opposition. Specifically, let us examine five truths about conquering our enemies by faith.

I. **Faith in God involves struggle**

If God promised a parcel of land to His people, wouldn't it have been easier to simply hand them an empty track of prime real estate? Why did the Israelites have to fight their way into a land that was already inhabited by a group of people? Fighting means struggle, and who in their right minds would ever voluntarily choose that route?

Let's face it, we all want the easy way out. Inventions are not merely reflections of human ingenuity, they are also commentaries on human slothfulness. We invent things to make life easier and to acquire our wants faster. Everything from microwave ovens to multi-capacity cell phones appeal to our love for what is easy. But God takes us to a place of struggle. What gives?

It is foolish to think that all struggle is senseless and that it yields nothing favorable. On the contrary, struggling breeds strength, perspective, and maturity that cannot be gained through mere handouts. Consider the story of the young lad who saw evidence of a butterfly prying its way out of a cocoon. Feeling sorry for the creature, the boy peeled the layers off the cocoon, thereby freeing the striving insect. Unfortunately, in his attempt to free the butterfly from its struggle, he actually deprived it of the opportunity to strengthen its wings which would have been necessary for it to fly. Instead, all the butterfly could do was crawl along the branch of the tree because, while it was once just an ugly caterpillar, it was now a beautiful butterfly . . . with a useless pair of wings.

Everything worth having is worth fighting for. Each day, we are compelled to choose our battles wisely. Some things are not worth an ounce of our energy, but other things are worth the very lives we live. The pursuit of God and His righteousness is one such thing. The people of Israel had to learn that if they were to enjoy the promises of God with wisdom, dignity, and an attitude to gratefulness, they would have to struggle their way to its fulfillment.

THE FAITH FACTOR

A person of faith understands that we struggle not to victory but from victory. The promises of God are sure and He, along with His promise, is the assurance that we already have what He pledged. Before the Israelites conquered the city of Jericho, the Lord said to Joshua, "I have given you Jericho, its king, and all its mighty warriors."[2] Notice how God used the past tense—"I have given you." For all practical purposes, the city of Jericho was already theirs, they simply had to step out in faith and receive it.

Are you deprived of a spiritual blessing because you refuse to exercise faith in the promises of God? If God has spoken it, it is already yours, not because of your faith, but because of His grace. The struggle of faith is simply the means by which God's promise is actualized in your life.

II. Faith in God involves obedience

The Lord works in mysterious ways—so cliché, and yet so true. God can sometimes be like that eccentric uncle whom you never quite understand, yet you are so drawn to. There is just something special about Him. At times you think you've figured it out, but just when you do, He throws a curve ball at you. For Joshua, the curve ball came in the form of a curious command.

After assuring Joshua of victory the Lord said,

> Your entire army is to march around the city once a day for six days. Seven priests will walk ahead of the Ark, each carrying a ram's horn. On the seventh day you are to march around the city seven times, with the priests blowing the horns. When

---

[2] Joshua 6:2

you hear the priests give one long blast on the horns, have all the people give a mighty shout. Then the walls of the city will collapse, and the people can charge straight into the city.[3]

Huh? Does that even make a little bit of sense to you? Let's see, a fortified city with massive double walls flanked by a world class fighting force stands between me and my promise, and God wants me to take a stroll and shout? Not exactly the combat strategy I would expect from a West Point training manual. Between you and me, I've shouted at buildings before and, trust me, they don't move. Yet, isn't that so like God? When have you known Him to do things conventionally? He asks Abraham to sacrifice his son, He asks Noah to build an ark on dry land, He leads the Israelites on a journey across the Red Sea, and now He is asking them to shout at a fortress.

Is God asking you to do something today that just doesn't make sense? You've done the math, checked it twice over, and nothing He says adds up. To obey or not to obey, that is the dilemma. The fact is, if you assume that the life of faith will always make perfect sense, then of what use is faith? Let me remind you that faith "is the confident assurance that what we hope for is going to happen . . . it is the evidence of things we cannot yet see."[4] With this in mind, what would you have done if you were Joshua?

The Bible says that Joshua listened to God's command, believed in the Lord, and obeyed as he was instructed. He acted in faith with no record of complaint or murmur. As a military professional, Joshua could have countered God's instruction with "better" suggestions. But spiritual victory depends on our

---

[3] Joshua 6:3-5
[4] Hebrews 11:1

THE FAITH FACTOR

obedience to God's way and will, not our own. And so even if His command may seem irrational—even foolish—we ought to obey just the same.

In *How Life Imitates the World Series*, Thomas Boswell recounts the story of the former manager of the Baltimore Orioles, Earl Weaver:

> Weaver had a rule that no one could steal a base unless given the signal sign. This upset Reggie Jackson because he felt he knew the pitchers and catchers well enough to judge who he could and could not steal off of. So one game he decided to steal without a sign. He got a good jump off the pitcher and easily beat the throw to second base. As he shook the dirt off his uniform, Jackson smiled with delight, feeling he had vindicated his judgment to his manager. Later, Weaver took Jackson aside and explained why he hadn't given the steal sign. First, the next batter was Lee May, his best power hitter other than Jackson. When Jackson stole second, first base was left open, so the other team walked May intentionally, taking the bat out of his hands. Second, the following batter hadn't been strong against that pitcher, so Weaver felt he had to send up a pinch hitter to try to drive in the men on base. That left Weaver without bench strength later in the game when he needed it.[5]

Reggie Jackson's problem was that he was only focusing on his relationship with the catcher while Weaver was focusing on the whole game. Weaver's actions were based on the overall plan of the game rather than its parts. In the same way, you and I tend to judge events only as they happen while God operates on a much grander scale. So what doesn't make sense to us makes perfect sense to Him. As people of faith, our challenge is to know Him

---

[5] Thomas Boswell, *How Life Imitates the World Series* (USA: Penguin Books, 1983).

well enough to acknowledge that He can be trusted and obeyed, even when the command makes no sense to us.

III. Faith in God involves trust

Obedience and trust go hand in hand. It is virtually impossible to have one without the other. When I was still a student, I took a flight to a town unfamiliar to me. My friend who lived in that town told me that as soon as I got off the plane, I was to meet him at the east wing of the airport. I did as he said on the basis of only one thing, I trusted him. It didn't matter that I was not familiar with the place or if the airport, indeed, had an east wing. It only mattered that my trusted friend told me that it was so and that he would be there to meet me.

We already agreed that God's command to march around Jericho was, shall we say, ludicrous. Yet one key element made all the difference for Joshua. The Bible says,

> After Joshua spoke to the people, the seven priests with the rams' horns started marching in the presence of the LORD, blowing the horns as they marched. And the priests carrying the Ark of the LORD's covenant followed behind them.[6]

Did you catch that? The priests started marching in the presence of the Lord. They had with them the Ark of the Covenant. This Ark represented God's presence. When the Ark was there God was there. No wonder they were willing to obey. They trusted that as long as God was with them, they had all they needed to see their promised victory.

---

[6] Joshua 6:8

The Faith Factor

It is so easy to forget about God's presence in the busyness of our daily lives. Too often, it seems that our schedules bombard us, enough to keep us busy that we no longer have time to enjoy our time with God. It is for this reason that we need Jericho moments. We need battles and struggles, if only to give God an opportunity to remind us that we are never left nor forgotten. We can trust Him because He is here.

Trust is developed over time. We grow in our ability to rely on God. At first, we might resist the invitation to surrender our lives to His care, but soon enough, we learn that He is truly trustworthy. In time, we cultivate a heart for His will and develop an ear to hear Him when He speaks. And at that opportune time, when He whispers in a small, still voice, we hear His command and instinctively respond in obedience and trust. Then we know we are maturing in our faith.

In 1976, over a hundred Israelis were held hostage by terrorists at the Entebbe Airport in Uganda. An elite group of Israeli soldiers set up a surprise attack to free the hostages and eliminate the terrorists. They had one problem. Both terrorists and hostages were in the same room, so how were they to take out the bad guys without harming their people? They found the perfect solution. As they entered the hostage site, the commander simply yelled, "Duck and take cover"—in Yiddish! Because the terrorists did not understand the language, only the Israelis ducked and took cover leaving the bad guys clear in the open. The strike force fired at those who remained standing, and soon the siege was over.

In times of crisis, are you able to hear God's voice amidst the other noises? Can you single out His Words enough to understand what He is saying to you? If so, then trust that what

He says is true and have faith that He only has your wellbeing in mind.

IV. Faith in God involves patience

You've probably seen the bumper sticker that reads, "Lord, I ask for patience and I want it right now!" This paradoxical prayer is all too reflective of our inability to wait on the promises of God. We may be willing to struggle, to obey, and to trust, but are we willing to wait? Thankfully, the Israelites showed that they were. The Bible says,

> Joshua got up early the next morning, and the priests again carried the ark of the LORD. The seven priests with the rams' horns marched in front of the Ark of the LORD, blowing their horns. Armed guards marched both in front of the priests with the horns and behind the Ark of the LORD. All this time the priests were sounding their horns. On the second day they marched around the city once and returned to the camp. They followed this pattern for six days.[7]

Based on the size of Jericho it would have taken the people about thirty minutes to march once around the nine-acre fortress. Consider, too, that the people were instructed to be quiet during these daily marches. Joshua said, "Do not shout; do not even talk . . . not a single word from any of you until I tell you to shout."[8] Do you realize what that meant? The Israelites were not given an opportunity to complain or murmur while they marched around Jericho. If they did, I wonder how many complainers would have ruined the whole experience.

---

[7] Joshua 6:12-14
[8] Joshua 6:10

The Faith Factor

When you are trusting in God, do yourself a favor and stay away from negative people. Don't listen to their senseless chatter and endless complaints because this will only work against your faith. Instead, surround yourself with faithful people: those who understand how dire a situation might be, yet are willing to put full trust in an all-powerful God and people who patiently wait for the right time for God's promises to be fulfilled.

Some of the greatest things in life do not come instantaneously. Cookies take time to bake, relationships take time to develop, skyscrapers take time to erect, and a child takes a whole nine months to show up! Yet nothing compares to the feeling of finally realizing what you have been waiting for. It is then that you know how it was well worth waiting for. In the same way, the patient people of Israel will learn soon enough how sweet God's victory really is.

Could it also be that God was purposely allowing the Israelites to be so physically spent that they had little strength left to fight the battle on their own? As they marched around the city once a day for six days, I can only imagine how tired they must have been. In a state of total exhaustion, we are left with no recourse but to trust in the strength of the Lord. With this, God was now ready to display His glory.

V.   Faith in God involves victory

Some have suggested that this story is one of the earliest records of psychological warfare in the ancient world. Can you imagine what the people of Jericho were thinking as the Israelites marched around them? They marched without speaking a word and without giving a clue as to how they planned to overpower the great fortified city. On the one hand, the people of Jericho may have thought, "These Hebrews are crazy; there is no way they will ever penetrate our walls." On the other hand, they might have thought, "Could they be concealing a secret weapon that we are completely oblivious to?" The mind-game would have been quite effective. In times of war, the element surprise is an excellent tool in the hands of the instigator. And the people of Jericho were in for the surprise of their lives.

On the seventh day, the Israelites marched around Jericho seven times. At the end of the seventh march, the Bible says,

> When the people heard the sound of the horns, they shouted as loud as they could. Suddenly, the wall of Jericho collapsed, and the Israelites charged straight into the city from every side and captured it![9]

With that shout, the Lord gave the Israelites their victory. The city was now theirs for the taking. In a sense, the audible shout was an outward expression of the Israelites' inward faith. While faith is primarily an internal matter of the soul, we express faith outwardly by proclaiming the praises of God in the midst of both friends and foe. Our cries of praise are declarations of victory and triumph given by the grace of Almighty God.

In the 1930s, archaeologist Dr. John Garstang made some interesting discoveries in the area believed to be the site of the ancient city of Jericho. He found pottery that showed a 1400 B.C. destruction of the city. The ruins also showed evidence that the surrounding wall did not fall flat on the ground but rather outward down the hillside, thereby dragging the inner wall and all the houses attached to it. The rest of the city was consumed

---

[9] Joshua 6:20

by fire. All of these findings are consistent with the victory story recorded in the sixth chapter of Joshua.

If you are longing for a spiritual victory in your life, do not ever tire of trusting in God and waiting on His perfect timing. As you exercise obedient faith, you will, in time, see the wonderful fulfillment of His promises. Then you will taste for yourself the sweet victory given only to those who put their trust in Him.

chapter

12

Rahab: Gracious Faith

*It was by faith that Rahab the prostitute did not die with
all the others in her city who refused to obey God.
For she had given a friendly welcome to the spies.*
(Hebrews 11:31)

If for some reason God decided to destroy the beautiful city of San Francisco and spare only one person, who do you suppose He would choose? Would any of you say He would save the local prostitute? Probably not. But that is exactly what the Lord did when He saved Rahab from the destruction of Jericho.

This story of redemption begins in the second chapter of Joshua. Think of it as the prequel of the Jericho saga. It is an amazing story of God's graciousness at a time when *grace* was not quite the theological buzzword it is today. Very often, the Old Testament conjures images of God's wrath and judgment and, indeed, there is no shortage of that. But intertwined in each judgment story is the story of God's mercy and grace.

The central character of the story is a woman named Rahab. She is described in Scripture as a harlot or a prostitute.

Not exactly the kind of person we associate with the holiness of God. Harlots were among the least favored people in any given society. They were scorned for their chosen profession and dismissed as detrimental to the spiritual climate of any town. But then again, what better person could there have been to demonstrate God's amazing grace? As Jesus reminded us, it is not the healthy people who need a doctor but the sick. Likewise, it is not the righteous who need a Savior but the sinner—and Rahab would have been counted among the chief of sinners. Imagine this, of all the people honored for their faith in Hebrews 11, the only woman mentioned was Rahab. Her special place in the Scripture's hall of faith is forever engraved in the inspired Word of God.

In this chapter, we will look into the events leading to the salvation of Rahab and the lessons of faith she provides for believers today.

I. Rahab's Redemption

Rahab encountered two Hebrew spies (Joshua 2:1-3). Before the attempt to conquer Jericho, Joshua sent two men to enter the city and spy out the land. Somehow, these men ended up in Rahab's house. It is possible that Rahab was walking through the city streets when she spotted the two men, possibly mistaking them for potential customers for the night. For whatever reason, the men trusted her enough to explain that they were spies and, therefore, needed some cover. Rahab graciously provided them with a place to stay. This unplanned meeting was the start of her redemption story.

Have you ever had a chance encounter with someone that turned out to be a divine appointment? When you meet someone, never underestimate the heights to which that encounter might result in. Many years ago, my mom's car was scraped by a truck resulting in some minor damages. The owner of the trucking company was kind enough to pay for the repairs. In the course of discussing the terms of the repair, the owner, a Christian, invited my mom to a Bible study meeting. This was the catalyst that eventually led her to accept Christ as Savior. Consequently, it was my mom who led the rest of our family to a saving knowledge of Jesus Christ. In a sense, I am a believer today because of an apparent chance meeting. Of course, you and I now know that God was in it all this time.

Rahab protected the two spies (Joshua 2:4-7). Word eventually got out that Hebrew spies had infiltrated Jericho and that they had encountered the harlot. When the king's officials questioned Rahab of the whereabouts of the spies, she distracted them by saying that the spies may have already left the city, after which the officials dispersed to pursue them. In reality, the spies were still hiding on the roof of Rahab's house. By distracting the king's men, Rahab protected the lives of the two spies.

Let me stop for a moment and address the elephant in the room. In her attempt to protect the spies, Rahab said, "The men were here earlier, but . . . I don't know where they went."[1] In other words, she lied, because she knew exactly where the spies were. But is her lie justified since she did it for a good reason? While it may be tempting to dismiss her lie in light of the greater good that was gained, we ought to be careful about making light of such an important moral issue because one of God's most important attributes is truth.

---

[1] Joshua 2:4-5

An important rule in biblical interpretation is to distinguish between what the Bible asserts versus what the Bible merely reports. In this case, while the Bible reports that Rahab lied, it does not assert that the lie was justifiable. Rahab was, indeed, esteemed enough to be included in the list of faithful people, but we must not assume that God approved everything she did. Walter Kaiser rightly contends,

> Rahab should have hidden the spies well and then refused to answer the question whether she was hiding them. She could, for instance, have volunteered, "Come in and have a look around," while simultaneously praying that God would make the searchers especially obtuse.[2]

Her lie was primarily an indication of her need to still mature in her young faith rather than a justification for speaking untruth when expedient.

Rahab appealed for mercy (Joshua 2:8-13). God was clearly on the side of the Israelites and Rahab knew it. She also knew that the destruction of Jericho was inevitable. In an act of utter desperation, she pleads for the spies to spare her and her family when the day of destruction comes. We can feel the passion of her plea in her words,

> Now swear to me by the LORD that you will be kind to me and my family since I have helped you. Give me some guarantee that when Jericho is conquered, you will let me live, along with my father and mother, my brothers and sisters, and all their families.[3]

---

[2] Walter C. Kaiser, Jr., *Hard Sayings of the Old Testament* (Downers Grove, IL: InterVarsity Press, 1988), p. 97.
[3] Joshua 2:12-13

THE FAITH FACTOR

God is near to the brokenhearted and has compassion to those who cry to Him for mercy. It was the writer of Hebrews who reminded us, "So let us come boldly to the throne of our gracious God. . . . There we will receive His mercy, and we will find grace to help us when we need it."[4] It has been said that *mercy* is when God does not give us what we deserve, while *grace* is when God gives us what we do not deserve. Thankfully, the Lord has never been known to turn away a penitent sinner, instead, He is known to be One who is rich in both mercy and grace.

Rahab was given the conditions for her rescue (Joshua 2:14-20). Before they left the city, the two spies assured Rahab and her family of safety. But there was one condition. They said,

> We can guarantee your safety only if you leave this scarlet rope hanging from the window. And all your family members . . . must be here inside the house. If they go out to the street, they will be killed, and we cannot be held to our oath. But we swear that no one inside this house will be killed—not a hand will be laid on any of them. If you betray us, however, we are not bound by this oath in any way.[5]

How fitting that the sign of their safety was a red rope draped over the window (Rahab's house was built into the city wall). The rope was a symbol that Rahab and her household were covered under God's protection and that they would be spared from the pending destruction of Jericho. Today, we are also given a red sign of God's protection—the blood of Jesus that covers our sins and washes them away. Those under the

---
[4] Hebrews 4:16
[5] Joshua 2:17-20

covering of Jesus' blood are promised eternal safety from the destructive forces of sin and death.

Rahab believed and was saved (Joshua 2:21; 6:22-23). With four simple words, "I accept your terms,"[6] Rahab sealed once for all her safety and that of her family. Her response was an act of faith. She did not ask for a detailed plan of how she would be rescued, or a written contract stipulating the terms of agreement; she simply trusted and believed.

Sometime later, when the moment of Jericho's fall came, God did not forget His promise. The Bible says that Joshua instructed the two spies, "Keep your promise. . . . Go to the prostitute's house and bring her out, along with all her family."[7] With that, Rahab and her family was not only rescued from danger, but was made to live as part of the Hebrew family. She was saved from destruction and adopted into the family of God's people.

Rahab would have one more important blessing. According to Matthew 1:5, she was part of the lineage through which Jesus the Messiah was to be born. Can you believe that? A Gentile prostitute, saved by the grace of God, became an ancestor of our Savior Jesus Christ! The grace of God is truly more than amazing.

II. The Lessons of Rahab's Faith

The life of Rahab is a lesson in gracious faith. In her experience, faith in God is met with the grace of God. We can

---

[6] Joshua 2:21
[7] Joshua 6:22

identify four important lessons from the faith experience of this great woman.

Faith is a non-discriminatory gift. Rahab was not a prominent member of Jericho's elite, she was a mere prostitute. Yet, she is forever known in Scripture as a woman of faith. The kingdom of God is made up of unlikely saints—sinners, just like you and me, who come to God in faith.

Faith comes by hearing. Rahab was able to believe because she heard the word regarding the works and power of God. When we do not take time to hear God's Word, we have no basis for belief. Conversely, when we hear the Word of God, we have the very foundation we need over which we are able to believe unto salvation.

Faith is evidenced by works. Rahab did not simply agree with the truth of God's Word, she acted on her belief by meeting the conditions for her rescue. Faith and works are like two oars needed to row a boat...without one, you will only travel in a circle. Together, they are a powerhouse through which the glory of God is revealed.

Faith brings about the fullness of God's blessings. Rahab only hoped to be spared from the city's destruction. But in the end, she enjoyed full fellowship with God's people. We often come to God for mundane things, only to realize that His desire for us is much more far-reaching. His desire is to be in fellowship with us for all eternity.

Rahab was spared from destruction because of the red rope that hung by her window. This red rope, typically a symbol of harlotry, is a symbol of the blood of Christ that brings redemption to all who believe. If you invoke the power of Christ's blood to cleanse you from sin and receive his sacrificial death as the payment for you offense, you will be saved. And

The Faith Factor

then you will fully appreciate the immortal words of the great hymn,

> Amazing Grace, how sweet the sound,
> that saved a wretch like me.
> I once was lost but now am found,
> was blind, but now, I see.

epilogue

The Next Hero of Faith
(Hebrews 11:32-12:2)

How you live your life today will determine how you will be remembered forever. The people honored in this book have gained that special place because they all chose to live by faith. They are our heroes of faith and the eleventh chapter of Hebrews stands as a memorial to their legacy. As we examine the final words of this great biblical chapter, let us look at what the author has to say about such heroes of faith.

I. Heroes of faith saturate biblical history.

> Well, how much more do I need to say? It would take too long to recount the stories of the faith of Gideon, Barak, Samson, Jephthah, David, Samuel, and all the prophets. By faith these people overthrew kingdoms, ruled with justice, and received what God had promised them. They shut the mouths of lions, quenched the flames of fire, and escaped death by the edge of the sword. Their weakness was turned to strength. They became strong in battle and put whole armies to flight. Women received their loved ones back again from death.
> (Hebrews 11:32-35a)

One Bible chapter is certainly not enough to discuss the lives of all the great heroes of faith found in Scripture. If you want to continue growing in faith, read the Bible! It is full of teachings, examples, and admonitions that will develop our faith in God.

THE FAITH FACTOR

If you have never done so, I encourage you to get into the habit of reading the Bible regularly. Too often, we rely on others to feed us, but a clear indication of maturity is the ability to feed yourself. Missionary Amy Carmichael once wrote, "Never let good books take the place of the Bible. . . . Drink from the Well, not from the streams that flow from the Well." The Bible is your spiritual food and God invites you to feast on it often.

II.   Heroes of faith paid a great price for their beliefs.

> But others trusted God and were tortured, preferring to die rather than turn from God and be free. They placed their hope in the resurrection to a better life. Some were mocked, and their backs were cut open with whips. Others were chained in dungeons. Some died by stoning, and some were sawed in half; others were killed with the sword. Some went about in skins of sheep and goats, hungry and oppressed and mistreated. They were too good for this world. They wandered over deserts and mountains, hiding in caves and holes in the ground.
> (Hebrews 11:35b-38)

The life of faith is not for the faint of heart. It takes a strong, committed person to endure the consequences of putting faith in the Lord God. While the Bible is full of stories that exemplify great faith, it also tells of those who have failed. Do you recall how Moses sent twelve spies to scout the Promised Land? Two gave a favorable report, while ten recommended that the Israelites retreat to a life of slavery. The names of the two faithful spies? Joshua and Caleb. The name of the other ten? We don't know and we don't care! If you do not live by faith, your name is not even worth remembering.

In the ancient Olympic Games, there was an event unlike any other. It was a foot race where the athletes ran while holding torches. The torches were lit at the beginning of the race and the winner was not the one who crossed the finish line, but the one who did so with their torch still lit. It is so easy to let the flame of our faith die in the course of living the Christian life. Let me remind you to keep your flame burning at any cost so that you will also enjoy the prize that is given to those who finish with their faith still ablaze.

III. Heroes of faith received blessings that were greater than they originally expected.

> All of these people we have mentioned received God's approval because of their faith, yet none of them received all that God had promised. For God had far better things in mind for us that would also benefit them, for they can't receive the prize at the end of the race until we finish the race.
> (Hebrews 11:39-40)

The biblical men and women of faith may have tasted some rewards, but their true reward for faith was eternal life with God. Don't be fooled into thinking that this life is all we have to live for. All we have today is temporary—everything soon fades away. Instead, we must keep our eyes on heavenly things where God's blessings will never cease.

In his book, *The Problem of Pain*, C. S. Lewis wrote,

> We are afraid that heaven is a bribe, and that if we make it our goal we shall no longer be disinterested. It is not so. Heaven offers nothing that a mercenary soul can desire. It is safe to tell

the pure in heart that they shall see God, for only the pure in heart want to.[1]

Lewis reminds us that the pursuit of heaven shall not disappoint because those of us who live by faith find our greatest reward in meeting the Author and Finisher of that faith. As if that was not enough, we will also meet the heroes of faith who have run ahead of us, and together, we will enjoy the fullness of the blessings of God in whom we have believed.

IV. Heroes of faith are cheering us on.

> Therefore, since we are surrounded by such a huge crowd of witnesses to the life of faith, let us strip off every weight that slows us down, especially the sin that so easily hinders our progress. And let us run with endurance the race that God has set before us. We do this by keeping our eyes on Jesus, on whom our faith depends from start to finish. He was willing to die a shameful death on the cross because of the joy he knew would be his afterward. Now he is seated in the place of highest honor beside God's throne in heaven.
>
> (Hebrews 12:1-2)

Although Hebrews eleven ends with verse forty, the discourse on faith carries on to chapter twelve. Here, the opening verses remind us that those who have run well are now seated in the stands cheering on those of us who are now running the race of faith. The heroes of faith make up our "crowd of witnesses." Although we may not hear their voices, the story of their lives are a resounding testimony that the race we run is well worth all the effort we put into it. If we look down, we will find

---

[1] C. S. Lewis, *The Problem of Pain* (New York: Macmillan, 1962), p. 145.

The Faith Factor

a beaten path marked with the footprints of those who have run faithfully before us. Do not look at these prints as obstacles but as guides leading to the race's end.

The story is told of a woman who trained hard to run in a famous city marathon. Confident that she had a chance to win, she drove to the city on the day of the race. Unfortunately, she did not anticipate all the festivities related to the marathon that she got stuck in traffic on the way there. Luckily, she got to the site just in time for the race to begin. She quickly signed it, attached her number to her shirt, and took her place at the starting point. At the sound of the gun, she began her first major marathon. Not only did she run, to her surprise, she actually won! Taking her place at the winner's stand, she was handed her prize—a water bottle and a commemorative T-shirt. How could this be? Surely the prize for a major city marathon was not a pair of cheap souvenirs.

To her horror, the woman soon realized that she ran the wrong race! Unbeknownst to her, alongside the real marathon was a mock-marathon organized for non-serious competitors. Because of the traffic fiasco, she parked on the wrong lot and signed up for the wrong marathon. All her training and effort amounted to nothing of worth.

Don't make the mistake of investing your time, energy, and faith in the wrong race. Run the race that God has set before you. Run it faithfully, and who knows—you may very well be the next hero of faith.

Now glory be to God! By his mighty power at work within us, he is able to accomplish infinitely more than we would ever dare to ask or hope. May he be given glory in the church and in Christ Jesus forever and ever through endless ages.
Amen
(Ephesians 3:20-21)

www.ingramcontent.com/pod-product-compliance
Lightning Source LLC
Chambersburg PA
CBHW072146160426
43197CB00012B/2265